HUNTING
THE
KILLER IDEA

Capturing the Creative Process

 *by*

NICK M^cFARLANE

I bring home this kill, to feed the ones I love.
Charlotte, Edie, May & Sid.

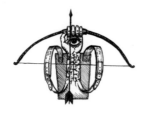

I'd like to sincerely thank the following people for their help and contribution towards the completion of this book.

CHARLOTTE McFARLANE
Thank you for your love and support throughout the journey. Transcribing interviews, putting up with my nightmares and holding the family together when the road got rough.

PETER VEGAS
For the final hunt, I called upon his skill and experience as a seasoned hunter, to help write and craft chapters 9 and 10.

MIKE BRAID
For the brilliant photography.

AUNTY JAN
For kindly transcribing the interviews.

SABINA BICKELMANN
For the editing and timely 11th hour advice.

A catalogue record for this book is available from the British Library. First Edition 2016. First published in Great Britain in 2016 by Carpet Bombing Culture. An imprint of Pro-actif Communications.

www.carpetbombingculture.co.uk | Email: books@carpetbombingculture.co.uk | © Carpet Bombing Culture. Pro-actif Communications

INTERVIEWS

LIAM HOWLETT
THE PRODIGY
– 86 –

NICK ONKEN
PHOTOGRAPHY
– 96 –

MARINA MUNN
ILLUSTRATION
– 88 –

COCO AND BREEZY
FASHION
– 106 –

MATT McATEER
POETRY
– 90 –

SACHA BARBER
AUTOMOTIVE DESIGN
– 108 –

ASKEW ONE
GRAFFITI
– 92 –

VINCE FROST
GRAPHIC DESIGN
– 112 –

CARLA ADAMS
ART
– 94 –

DAVE TROTT
ADVERTISING
– 122 –

And a brief Q&A with

NOAM CHOMSKY
ANARCHIST
– 150 –

JOURNEY OF PAGES

→

- 1 -
INTO THE WILD

Planning and preparation before the hunt.

10 – 27

- 2 -
BIG GAME HUNTERS

Hunting big ideas, using philosophical thinking.

28 – 45

- 3 -
HUNTER GATHERERS

Observing and foraging for ideas in their natural environment.

46 – 63

- 4 -
MOUNTAIN GUIDES

Conquering the creative challenge.

64 – 81

- 5 -
CULTURE CATCHERS

Searching the soul and hunting for inspiration.

82 – 99

JOURNEY OF PAGES

- 6 -
TRAPPERS
Trapping ideas to inform great design.

100 — 117

- 7 -
HEAD HUNTERS
Turning heads and touching hearts through advertising.

118 — 135

- 8 -
SURVIVALISTS
Surviving the harshest conditions.

136 — 153

- 9 -
THE HUNT
The Killer Idea is hunted.

154 — 183

- 10 -
THE KILL
Executing the Killer Idea.

184 — 197

Of course it won't be easy.

Nothing worthwhile ever is.

- SURVIVAL KIT & HUNTING WITS

CREATIVE PROCESS

GUIDE TO HUNTING

INTO

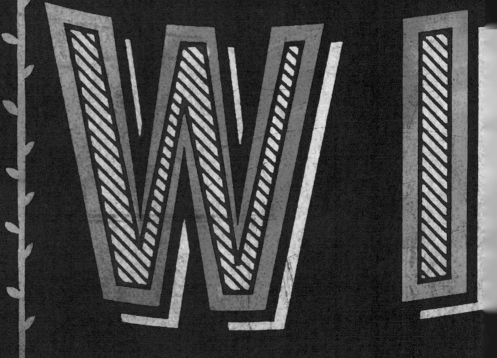

W |

- KNOW THYSELF · GRIT'N G

E INFINITY OF IMAGINATION •

THE

LD

ON • THE BAG OF ABILITY •

KNOW
THYSELF

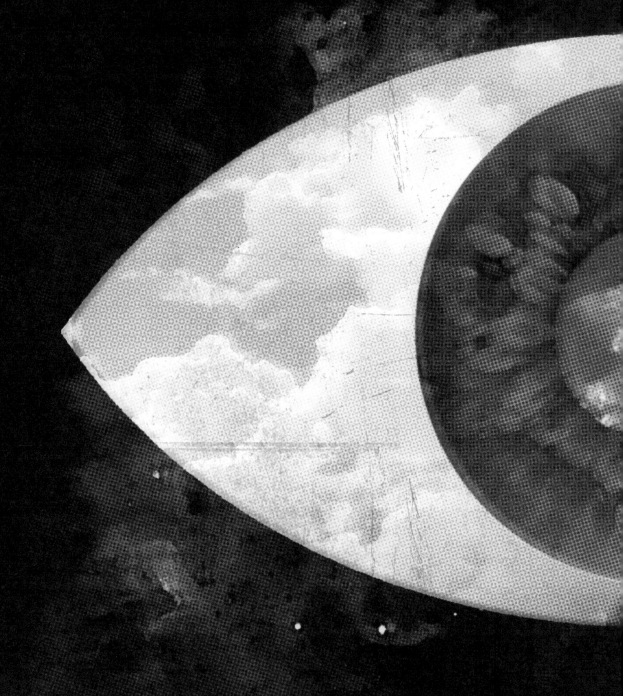

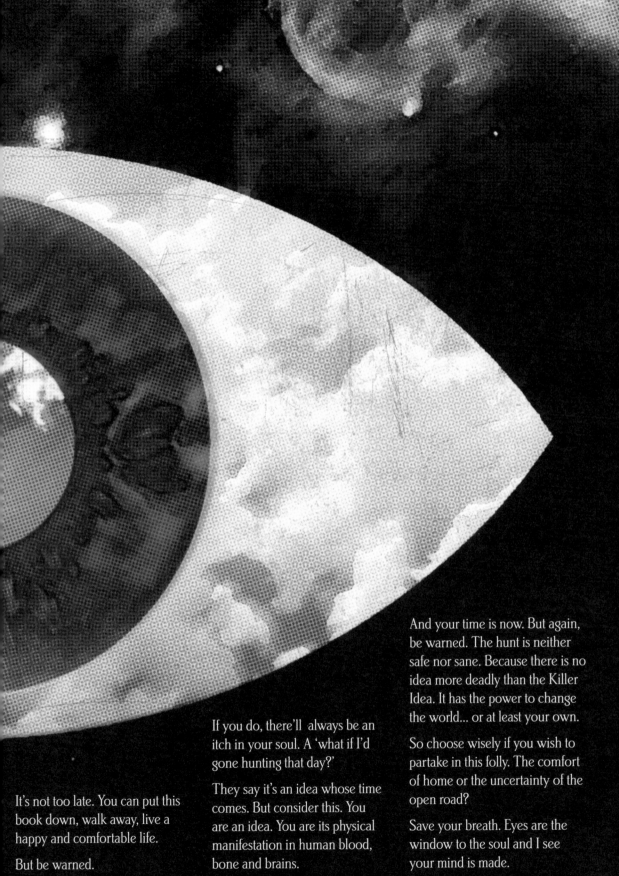

And your time is now. But again, be warned. The hunt is neither safe nor sane. Because there is no idea more deadly than the Killer Idea. It has the power to change the world... or at least your own.

So choose wisely if you wish to partake in this folly. The comfort of home or the uncertainty of the open road?

If you do, there'll always be an itch in your soul. A 'what if I'd gone hunting that day?'

They say it's an idea whose time comes. But consider this. You are an idea. You are its physical manifestation in human blood, bone and brains.

Save your breath. Eyes are the window to the soul and I see your mind is made.

It's not too late. You can put this book down, walk away, live a happy and comfortable life.

But be warned.

GRIT 'N GUMPTION

Good for you.

Well let's begin with the absolute basics of what you'll be needing.

If ambition's the fire in the belly that keeps you warm at night, grit's the last ember from your dying self belief that refuses to go out when the cold winds blow.

From this final spark can be lit one last fire to at least see you through to dawn. Because who knows what tomorrow may bring?

Grit's the courage to ignore the common sense of the crowd and pursue one's own direction in life. Grit's what forces you to rack your brains one last time.

Gumption's what killed the cat. Gumption's what makes you tick. Makes you want to ask why? Why not? Why not now? Gumption's the ingenuity which is at the heart of all creative endeavours and grit's what keeps it going when a lost cause is all it looks like you might catch.

Because the thing is, ideas are beautiful. But when they're just beginning out in the world they're delicate and easily broken. Corrupted. Squashed. Humiliated for being strange.

New ideas are often ridiculed for not fitting in with the way things are meant to be done, as the old order tries to protect its turf.

Humans are naturally inquisitive creatures. And it's our curiosity to understand the world and our part in the larger scheme of things which fuels the creative process.

So when you're unsure of the best way forward, grit your teeth and have the gumption to never stop asking questions.

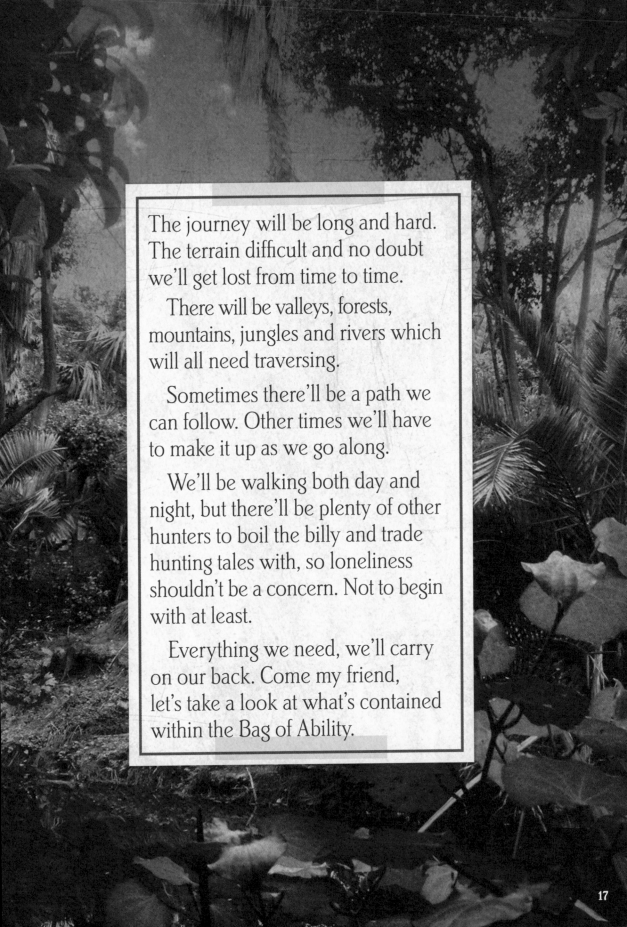

The journey will be long and hard. The terrain difficult and no doubt we'll get lost from time to time.

There will be valleys, forests, mountains, jungles and rivers which will all need traversing.

Sometimes there'll be a path we can follow. Other times we'll have to make it up as we go along.

We'll be walking both day and night, but there'll be plenty of other hunters to boil the billy and trade hunting tales with, so loneliness shouldn't be a concern. Not to begin with at least.

Everything we need, we'll carry on our back. Come my friend, let's take a look at what's contained within the Bag of Ability.

SURVIVAL KIT & HUNTING WITS {Attributes & Aptitude}

CONTAINED WITHIN THE BAG OF ABILITY IS EVERYTHING YOU'LL NEED TO HUNT THE KILLER IDEA AND SURVIVE IN THE WILDERNESS.

Indeed, you've possessed most of these items during your life. Sometimes trading up or adding to the stock.

Each item here represents an attribute which makes up the equipment in your survival kit.

Out in the wild this is more or less all you'll have to rely on. If you're hoping to be successful you'll need quick wits when using your kit. In other words, how fast can you think on your feet?

It's a useful exercise now to lay everything out. Check the blades are sharp, matches dry and compass pointing North.

In daily life you can get by with blunt, frayed and faulty equipment. But not now. Not if you're to be the hunter rather than the hunted.

Let's mull over the qualities which several of these items lend. But keep in mind the sum is always greater than its parts.

BOW & ARROW (01.-02.)
The embodiment of judgment and accuracy. With good judgment you can appraise the distance required to strike a target and whether it is within your range or not. With accuracy you can confidently hit problems between the eyes from a safe distance.

GRAPPLING ROPE (06.)
Scaling great heights or escaping out of the creative abyss requires strength and determination.

TREASURE BOX (07.)
Used for the storing of memories. In here, your thoughts are locked away to be examined at a later date.

MACHETE (09.)
Perseverance is what you'll need for the hard work of hacking through the dense foliage which inevitably slows progress.

COMPASS (17.)
Providing a sense of direction, which in turn gives you certainty. Without it you're as good as lost.

HUNTING HORN (18.)
Representing language, the horn is traditionally used to signal one's position and communicate intentions in the hunt.

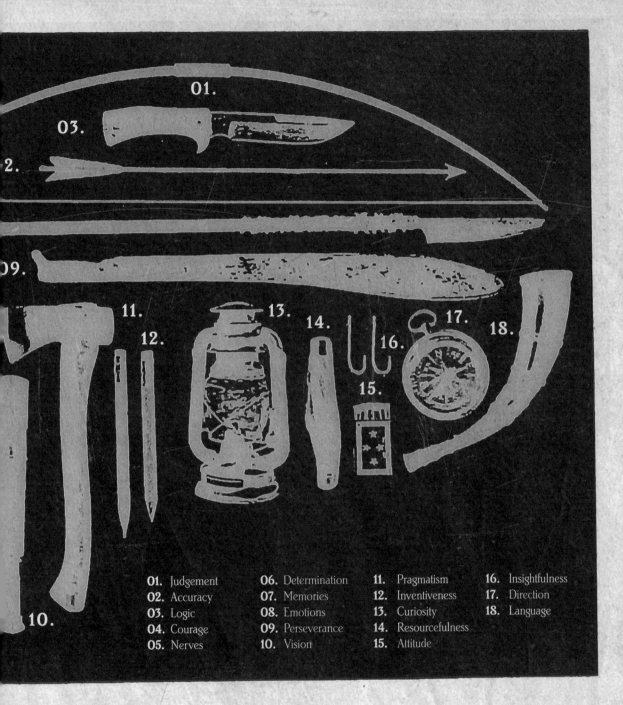

01. Judgement
02. Accuracy
03. Logic
04. Courage
05. Nerves
06. Determination
07. Memories
08. Emotions
09. Perseverance
10. Vision
11. Pragmatism
12. Inventiveness
13. Curiosity
14. Resourcefulness
15. Attitude
16. Insightfulness
17. Direction
18. Language

SHARPENING STONE (05.)

Nerves have a funny habit of popping up just when you want them least. Most folk think that's a bad thing. The mere thought of what's coming is enough to make you turn your back and walk away. But the seasoned hunter understands the purpose of nerves. For if understood correctly, nerves are the stone upon which your wits are sharpened. With a sharp mind, one is far more effective. So when beads of sweat form upon your brow, skin goes clammy and heart beat quickens. Fear not the attacking nerves, instead embrace the fact that you're fully alert and focused. A sharp blade means a quick kill. ♣

There is one thing however, which is not depicted as part of your survival kit, yet without it all of these items are useless.

The good news is, if you can guess what it is, youre already using it.

THE INFINITY OF
IMAGINATION

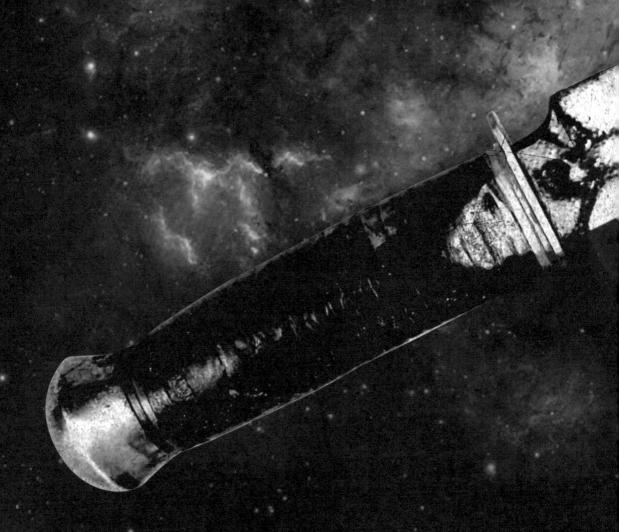

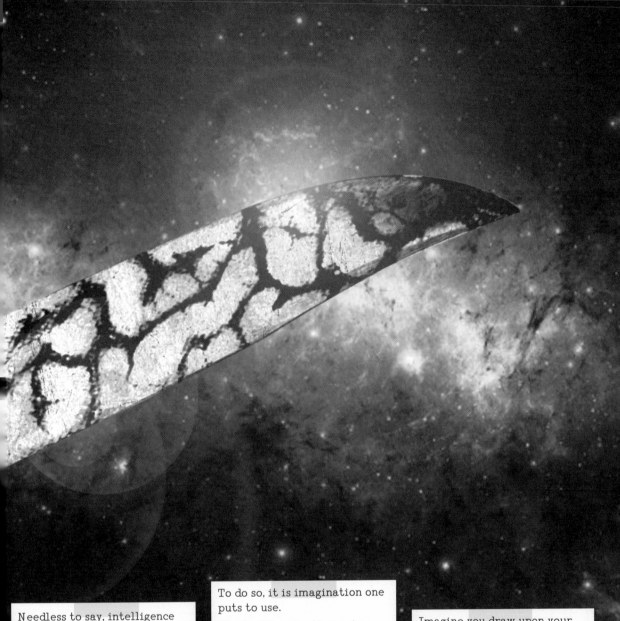

Needless to say, intelligence is important - you won't get far without a smart head upon your shoulders.

But acumen merely provides a sharp edge to the mind. Unless it's wielded deftly and handled with skill, it'll serve no greater purpose.

When you set your mind to the hunt you'll not only need a wide array of weapons and equipment. You'll also need to gain mastery over how each item is used.

To do so, it is imagination one puts to use.

Think of imagination not as something found in your survival kit, but instead as the action of reaching in and selecting the right item for the right situation - in the process bringing your hunting wits to life.

If you're quick witted it'll be drawn at speed. If you've a wild imagination, what you draw upon and how you use it will be unexpected. Not only giving you the element of

Imagine you draw upon your hunting knife. The blade can be put to many different uses.

It can be used to carve the initials of a loved one into a tree. To remove a thorn from the paw of a fellow hunting companion. Or indeed to execute the Killer Idea.

Imagination cuts open a hole in the blackness of the universe, letting in the light from an infinite number of stars. ✤

THE KILLER IDEA

AND OTHER CREATIVE ODDITIES.

OUT IN THE WILD THERE ARE MANY STRANGE VARIETIES OF IDEAS WHICH ONE MAY CHANCE UPON. SOME ARE CRAZY, OTHERS CLEVER. BUT THE KIND WE'RE AFTER IS KNOWN AS THE KILLER IDEA.

The Killer Idea is wildly imaginative, beastly in size, of sharp intelligence and creative in application.

Its capture is always shocking as a new and previously unknown human truth becomes visible for all to see.

They're called Killer Ideas because they change the way we see the world. In other words, they kill off previously held beliefs. Destroy weaker ideas and in the process give birth to entirely new mind sets. By their very nature they're impossible to predict, difficult to track yet as delicate as they are deadly.

They break barriers, upend order, savage sanity and force everyone to re-evaluate the workings of the world. Their effects reverberate and echo across the ages.

They stand in front of us all, yet hide from plain sight. When captured, their truth and meaning is declared as being blindingly obvious by all.

In their natural habitat the rules of logic cease to make sense. For the hunter entering the terrain - where madness and genius are hard to distinguish between - there are many dangers present.

Some of the most powerful Killer Ideas were captured centuries

ago by people known in common parlance as philosophers. But in these pages we refer to them as Big Game Hunters.

Their ideas have shaped much of Western Civilisation, so it is important that we visit their thoughts first in order to understand the significance of logic and reason. ❖

Observe the tracks and spoors yonder if you will. And also the map overleaf, which details the terrain you'll be tackling. Righto, sling y'r bag over shoulder, it's into the wild we go.

THE CREATIVE PROCESS (AS THE CROW FLIES)

THE IMPASSE
CREATIVE CHALLENGE
HIGHS
VISION
THE VILLAGE
GATHERING OBSERVATIONS
FIRST THOUGHTS
WILD OPEN
FEAR
LOWS
VERIFICATION
THE KILL

DIAGRAM NOT TO SCALE

DIFFERENT TYPES OF CREATIVE ENDEAVOUR.

OBSERVE HOW VARIABLE CONDITIONS DETERMINE THE APPROACH.

HIGH CREATIVITY	**EXPEDITION** This is an enjoyable type of hunt, rambling along, exploring less obvious opportunities, stopping to appreciate the view. Safe in the knowledge the family back in the village is comfortable and well fed.	**HUNTING** Creativity loves constraint as it forces the hunter to be thoughtful, to prioritize needs over wants and to be as innovative as possible. The pressure forces focus, meaning the terrain is researched and the prey defined.
LOW CREATIVITY	**RAMBLE** Without incentive or encouragement the hunt becomes boring and pointless. Feeling uninspired and without purpose the hunter won't spot opportunities, let alone capture creativity in any decent form.	**UPHILL BATTLE** When the pressure to feed the village is unrelenting, yet those leading the party are unfocused, and the objectives keep changing, the hunter is likely to feel like they're battling uphill but never reaching the top.
	LOW PRESSURE	**HIGH PRESSURE**

SOURCE: Creativity Under the Gun, Teresa Amabile, Constance Hadley, Steve Kramer

TABLE OF PREY

TRACKS, SPOORS & DESCRIPTIONS OF IDEAS FOUND IN THE CEREBRAL KINGDOM

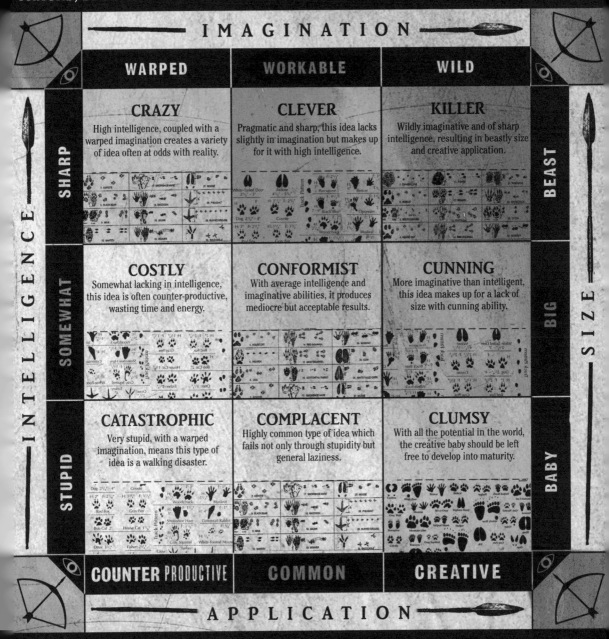

IMAGINATION

	WARPED	WORKABLE	WILD	
SHARP	**CRAZY** — High intelligence, coupled with a warped imagination creates a variety of idea often at odds with reality.	**CLEVER** — Pragmatic and sharp, this idea lacks slightly in imagination but makes up for it with high intelligence.	**KILLER** — Wildly imaginative and of sharp intelligence, resulting in beastly size and creative application.	**BEAST**
SOMEWHAT	**COSTLY** — Somewhat lacking in intelligence, this idea is often counter-productive, wasting time and energy.	**CONFORMIST** — With average intelligence and imaginative abilities, it produces mediocre but acceptable results.	**CUNNING** — More imaginative than intelligent, this idea makes up for a lack of size with cunning ability.	**BIG**
STUPID	**CATASTROPHIC** — Very stupid, with a warped imagination, means this type of idea is a walking disaster.	**COMPLACENT** — Highly common type of idea which fails not only through stupidity but general laziness.	**CLUMSY** — With all the potential in the world, the creative baby should be left free to develop into maturity.	**BABY**
	COUNTER PRODUCTIVE	**COMMON**	**CREATIVE**	

INTELLIGENCE (left axis) — **SIZE** (right axis)

APPLICATION

GATHERING OF RESOURCES. Raw materials relating to creativity. (And what to avoid).

KNOWLEDGE	**ATTITUDE**	**IMAGINATION**	**POISONS**
Gaining energy and sustenance from natural resources.	Adding your inner spark to creative kindling.	Creating an environment nurturing of new ideas.	Beware of certain ideas or attitudes containing negativity.

THE
VILLAGE

COMFORT ZONE

FREE RANGES

-1-
INTO
THE
WILD

FIRST THOUGHTS

GENTLE STREAM

-2-
BIG GAME
HUNTING

OPEN VALLEY

THE WILDERNES

N

-3-
HUNTER
GATHERERS

THE BLACK LAKE OF THE
SUBCONSCIOUS MIND

THE
GREAT
IMPASSE

MAP OF THE
CEREBRAL KINGDOM
WITHIN WHICH THE KILLER IDEA IS THOUGHT TO HIDE
— — — — And also showing the Hunters' journey of pages — — — —

The journey is the destination.

Into the wild we go.

Roam through rain,
sleet and snow.
To gather the things
we ought to know.
Into the wild we go.

Some say it unwise
to march on unknown skies.
But the most foolish thing
that could happen to you.
Is to not do the things
you were born to do.

So, into the wild we go.

BIG
GA
HUN

ME

TERS

PAW PRINT
OF PHILOSOPHY

MANY DANGEROUS BEASTS ARE TO BE FOUND IN THE WILD, SO BEFORE VENTURING TOO FAR IT'D BE WISE TO PONDER THE SIGNIFICANCE OF THIS PRINT.

Over the ages there have been all sorts of hunters who have dedicated their lives searching tirelessly in the darker corners of the human psyche for answers to life's big questions.

Philosophy, meaning "love of wisdom" involves a systematic approach to thinking that relies on rational argument as the primary method for not only capturing ideas, but exploring and questioning the meaning of the concepts which underpin the things we assume we know for sure.

From early hunters such as Socrates, who claimed to be the wisest of all because he knew he knew nothing and chose a death sentence of poison over renouncing knowledge and accepting ignorance.

JUST AS HUNTING IS NOT ONLY ABOUT THE KILL PHILOSOPHY IS NOT ONLY ABOUT ANSWERS MORE IMPORTANTLY IT IS ABOUT THE PROCESS OF FINDING THESE ANSWERS

HUMAN BEINGS ARE NATURALLY INQUISITIVE CREATURES TO CAPTURE THE TRUTH WE USE REASON WHENEVER WE REASON WE ARE THINKING (HUNTING) PHILOSOPHICALLY

To civil rights leaders and everyone else in between who have applied critical thinking and reason, to make sense of the world we live in.

THE PHILOSOPHICAL HUNTER SEEKS ANSWERS WHICH HAVE RATIONAL JUSTIFICATIONS

THE PHILOSOPHICAL HUNTER QUESTIONS & CHALLENGES IGNORANCE TRADITIONAL AUTHORITY CONVENTIONS ASSUMPTIONS UNKNOWNS DOGMA

THE PHILOSOPHICAL HUNTER USES LOGIC & LANGUAGE AS PRIMARY WEAPONS.

EAS ARE CAPTURED USING EXAMINATION, ARGUMENT & COUNTER-ARGUMENT & OUR ITELLECTUAL CAPACITY TO REASON

H LEADS TO TRUTH LEADS TO TRUTH LEADS TO TRUTH LEADS TO A LOGICAL CONCLUSION

THE BIG QUESTIONS:

HAT IS EXISTENCE? WHAT IS THE NATURE OF EXISTENCE? (ONTOLOGY) WHAT IS THE UNIVERSE MADE OF? METAPHYSICS

NSCIOUSNESS

KNOWLEDGE? WHAT IS IT? (EPISTEMOLOGY) HOW CAN WE REALLY KNOW WHAT WE KNOW?

Their combined effort to hunt big ideas has resulted in success and failure over the centuries, but what has at least been recorded is this print, giving an indication of the size of the challenge associated with Big Game Hunting.✤

THE BIG FIVE

BELOW ARE THE FIVE BIGGEST QUESTIONS WHICH PHILOSOPHERS HAVE BEEN CHASING. FROM ALL DIFFERENT ANGLES, HUNTERS HAVE TRIED TO TACKLE THESE BEASTS, ATTEMPTING TO PIN DOWN THEIR ILLUSIVE QUALITIES.

1. WHAT'S OUT THERE?

METAPHYSICS: What is the universe made of? And for that matter, what is the nature of whatever it is that exists? This includes everything from the stars in the heavens to the atoms in your finger tips. Not to mention the thoughts in your head. So what is the relationship between body, mind and soul?

2. HOW DO I KNOW WHAT I KNOW?

EPISTEMOLOGY: How do we acquire knowledge? And how can we be sure of what we know, if we only have our senses to rely on? Is knowledge innate? Or do we learn everything from our experiences in life? Since we're hunting for the truth, we also need to know what the limits of human knowledge are?

3. WHAT SHOULD I DO?

ETHICS: What is right? What is wrong? What is the best way for people to live? What is a "good" life? What do Justice and Happiness actually mean? Hold on tight, because the hunt gets a whole lot trickier when we begin to ask what actions are right or wrong, and does that change under certain circumstances?

4. WHAT ACTIONS ARE PERMISSIBLE?

POLITICS: How should humans, communities, nations best be organised, controlled and governed? Politics is also the study and practice of the distribution of power and resources within a given community. What rights and responsibilities should the citizens have? Or not have?

5. WHAT CAN LIFE BE LIKE?

AESTHETICS: What can be considered beautiful? Is it really in the eye of the beholder? This beast deals with the notions of art, beauty and taste. And how culture and society influence our perception and understanding of these concepts. As art is a reflection of not only culture, but life itself.

COGITO ERGO SUM

FROM THE DAWN OF CIVILISATION UNTIL THE PRESENT DAY, THESE BEASTS HAVE BEEN TRACKED AND HUNTED IN THE PURSUIT OF TRUTH AND KNOWLEDGE. MANY A SPEAR HAS BEEN HURLED THEIR WAY. HERE ARE BUT A FEW.

EXISTENCE
METAPHYSICS

NOTHING COMES FROM NOTHING, THEREFORE EXISTENCE IS ETERNAL
PARMENIDES

HAPPINESS IS THE MEANING AND PURPOSE OF LIFE, THE WHOLE AIM AND END OF HUMAN EXISTENCE

TRUTH RESIDES IN THE WORLD AROUND US
ARISTOTLE

ANXIETY IS THE DIZZINESS OF FREEDOM
SØREN KIERKEGAARD

EVERY PERSON TAKES THE LIMITS OF THEIR OWN FIELD OF VISION FOR THE LIMITS OF THE WORLD
ARTHUR SCHOPENHAUER

LIFE IS A SERIES OF COLLISIONS **WITH THE FUTURE**
JOSE ORTEGA Y GASSET

A THING ONLY EXISTS IN SO FAR AS IT PERCEIVES OR IS PERCEIVED
GEORGE BERKLEY

THE WORLD IS, OF COURSE, NOTHING **BUT OUR CONCEPTION OF IT**
ANTON CHEKHOV

KNOWLEDGE
EPISTEMOLOGY

THE UNEXAMINED LIFE IS NOT WORTH LIVING

THE ONLY TRUE WISDOM IS IN KNOWING YOU KNOW NOTHING
SOCRATES

COGITO ERGO SUM

I THINK
THEREFORE I AM
RENE DESCARTES

DOUBT IS NOT A PLEASANT CONDITION, **BUT CERTAINTY IS ABSURD**
VOLTAIRE

THOUGHT HAS ALWAYS WORKED BY OPPOSITION
HELENE CIXOUS

EDUCATION IS NOT PREPARATION FOR LIFE; EDUCATION IS LIFE ITSELF
JOHN DEWEY

KNOWLEDGE IS POWER
FRANCIS BACON

THERE IS NOTHING IN THE MIND EXCEPT WAS FIRST IN THE SENSES
JOHN LOCKE

ACTION
ETHICS

FORCE
POLITICS

ART
AESTHETICS

IF WE CHOOSE, WE CAN LIVE IN A WORLD OF COMFORTING ILLUSIONS

NOAM CHOMSKY

THOSE WHO CANNOT REMEMBER THE PAST ARE CONDEMNED TO REPEAT IT

GEORGE SANTAYANA

THE GOOD LIFE IS ONE INSPIRED BY LOVE AND GUIDED BY KNOWLEDGE

BERTRAND RUSSELL

ANYBODY CAN BECOME ANGRY – THAT IS EASY, BUT TO BE ANGRY WITH THE RIGHT PERSON AND TO THE RIGHT DEGREE AND AT THE RIGHT TIME AND FOR THE RIGHT PURPOSE, AND IN THE RIGHT WAY – THAT IS NOT WITHIN EVERYBODY'S POWER AND IS NOT EASY

ARISTOTLE

HE HAS THE MOST WHO IS MOST CONTENT WITH THE LEAST

DIOGENES OF SINOPE

GENUINE TRAGEDIES IN THE WORLD ARE NOT CONFLICTS BETWEEN RIGHT AND WRONG. THEY ARE CONFLICTS **BETWEEN TWO RIGHTS**

GEORG HEGAL

ETHICS IS KNOWING THE DIFFERENCE **BETWEEN WHAT YOU HAVE** A RIGHT TO DO AND WHAT IS RIGHT TO DO

POTTER STEWART

MAN IS BORN FREE, YET EVERYWHERE HE IS IN CHAINS

JEAN-JACQUES ROUSSEAU

MAN IS AN ANIMAL THAT MAKES BARGAINS

ADAM SMITH

THE HISTORY OF ALL HITHERTO EXISTING SOCIETY IS THE HISTORY OF CLASS STRUGGLES

THE RULING IDEAS OF EACH AGE HAVE EVER BEEN THE IDEAS OF ITS RULING CLASS

KARL MARX

EVERY DESIRE HAS A RELATIONSHIP TO MADNESS

LUCE IRIGARAY

THE ONE WHO ADAPTS HIS POLICY TO THE TIMES PROSPERS, AND LIKEWISE THAT THE ONE WHOSE POLICY CLASHES WITH THE DEMANDS OF THE TIMES DOES NOT

NIICCOLO MACHIAVELLI

THE GREATEST GOOD FOR THE GREATEST NUMBER
JEREMY BENTHAM

ONE OF THE PENALTIES FOR REFUSING TO PARTICIPATE IN POLITICS IS THAT YOU END UP BEING GOVERNED **BY YOUR INFERIORS**

PLATO

THE AIM OF ART IS TO REPRESENT NOT THE OUTWARD APPEARANCE OF THINGS, BUT THEIR INWARD SIGNIFICANCE

ARISTOTLE

BEAUTY IS WITHIN THE SUBJECT, NOT THE OBJECT

IMMANUEL KANT

ART IS A FORM OF LIFE

RICHARD WOLLHEIM

I THINK OF ART, AT ITS MOST SIGNIFICANT, AS A DEW LINE, A DISTANT EARLY WARNING SYSTEM THAT CAN ALWAYS BE RELIED ON TO TELL THE OLD CULTURE WHAT IS BEGINNING TO **HAPPEN TO IT**

MARSHALL MCLUHAN

ART IS A HUMAN ACTIVITY CONSISTING IN THIS, THAT ONE MAN CONSCIOUSLY, BY MEANS OF CERTAIN EXTERNAL SIGNS, HANDS ON TO OTHERS FEELINGS HE HAS LIVED THROUGH, AND THAT OTHER PEOPLE ARE INFECTED BY THESE FEELINGS AND **ALSO EXPERIENCE THEM**

TOLSTOY

THE BEST PART OF BEAUTY IS THAT WHICH NO PICTURE CAN EXPRESS

FRANCIS BACON

LOVE OF BEAUTY IS TASTE. THE CREATION OF BEAUTY IS ART

RALPH WALDO EMERSON

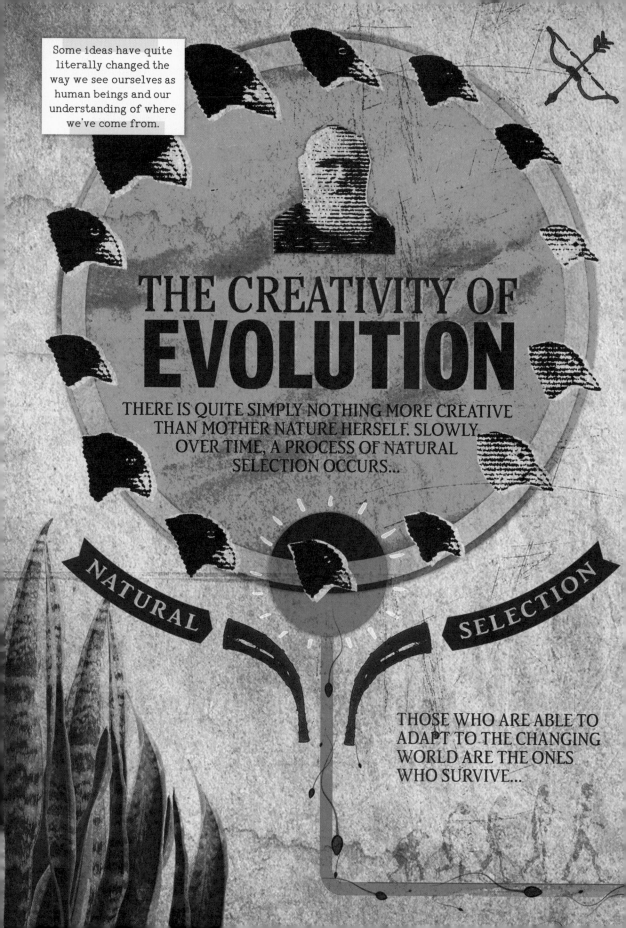

Some ideas have quite literally changed the way we see ourselves as human beings and our understanding of where we've come from.

THE CREATIVITY OF
EVOLUTION

THERE IS QUITE SIMPLY NOTHING MORE CREATIVE THAN MOTHER NATURE HERSELF. SLOWLY, OVER TIME, A PROCESS OF NATURAL SELECTION OCCURS...

NATURAL   SELECTION

THOSE WHO ARE ABLE TO ADAPT TO THE CHANGING WORLD ARE THE ONES WHO SURVIVE...

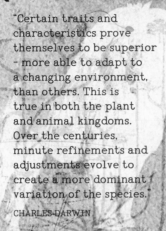

"Certain traits and characteristics prove themselves to be superior - more able to adapt to a changing environment, than others. This is true in both the plant and animal kingdoms. Over the centuries, minute refinements and adjustments evolve to create a more dominant variation of the species."

CHARLES DARWIN

IT IS NOT THE STRONGEST OF THE SPECIES THAT SURVIVE, NOR THE MOST INTELLIGENT, BUT THE ONES MOST RESPONSIVE TO CHANGE
~ CHARLES DARWIN ~

SURVIVAL
OF THE FITTEST

THE FORM THAT WILL LEAVE THE MOST COPIES OF ITSELF IN SUCCESSIVE GENERATIONS.

The hunter would do well to observe certain principles and apply them back to their own creative process. Namely adaptability (not to mention patience).

Charles Darwin captured this idea, with the publication of On Natural Selection in 1859, after observing evidence of how populations evolve over the course of generations through a process of natural selection.

And so it is with ideas. Will it replicate? Will it be shared? Will it survive, whilst others become obsolete, unimportant or even die? This becomes a useful tool in evaluating if an idea is killer or not. ❖

How does philosophy work in the real world? Gandhi was able to force the British empire out of India using a philosophy of non-violent civil disobedience.

His teachings are also of value to the creative process in general.

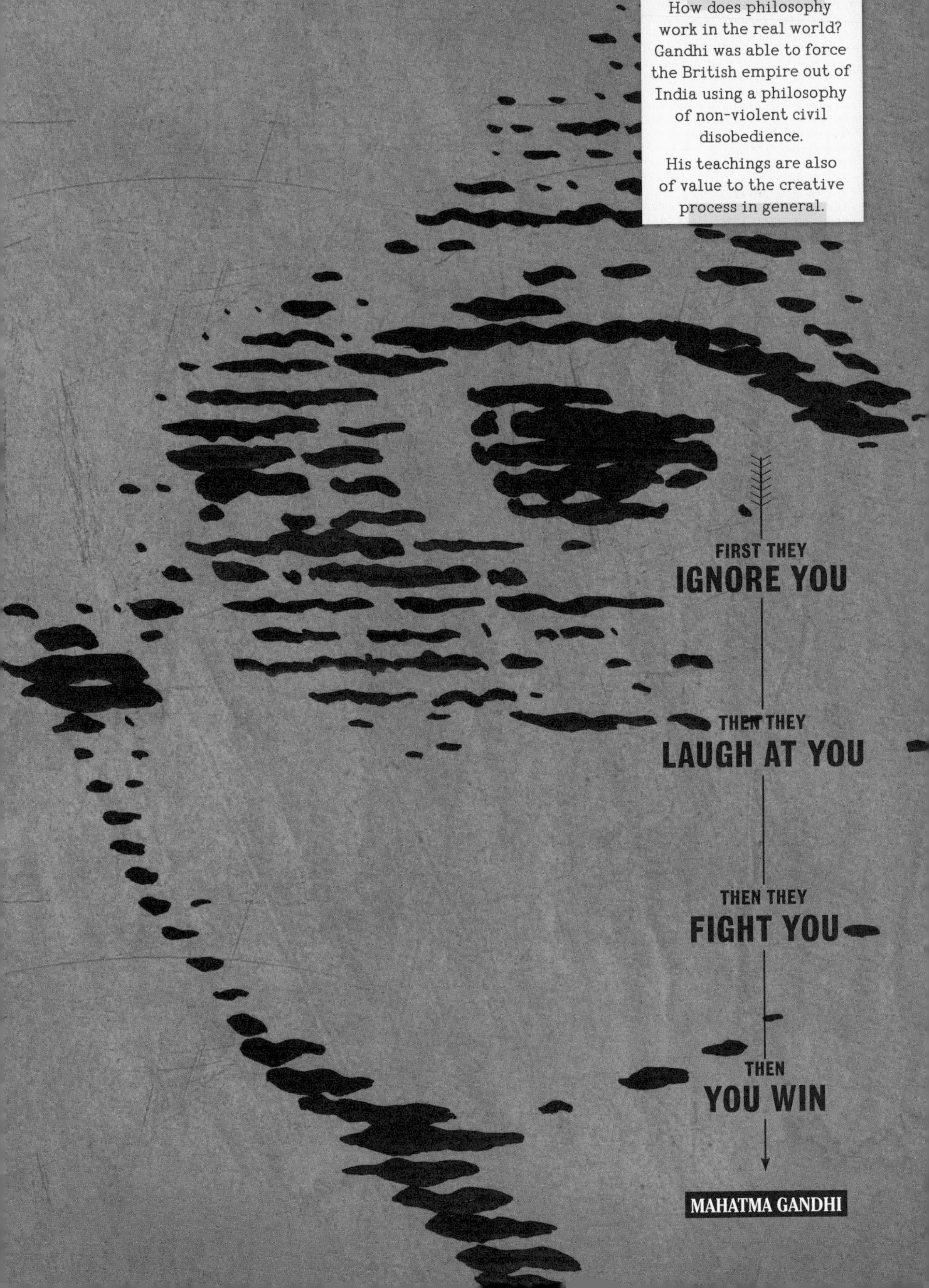

FIRST THEY
IGNORE YOU

THEN THEY
LAUGH AT YOU

THEN THEY
FIGHT YOU

THEN
YOU WIN

MAHATMA GANDHI

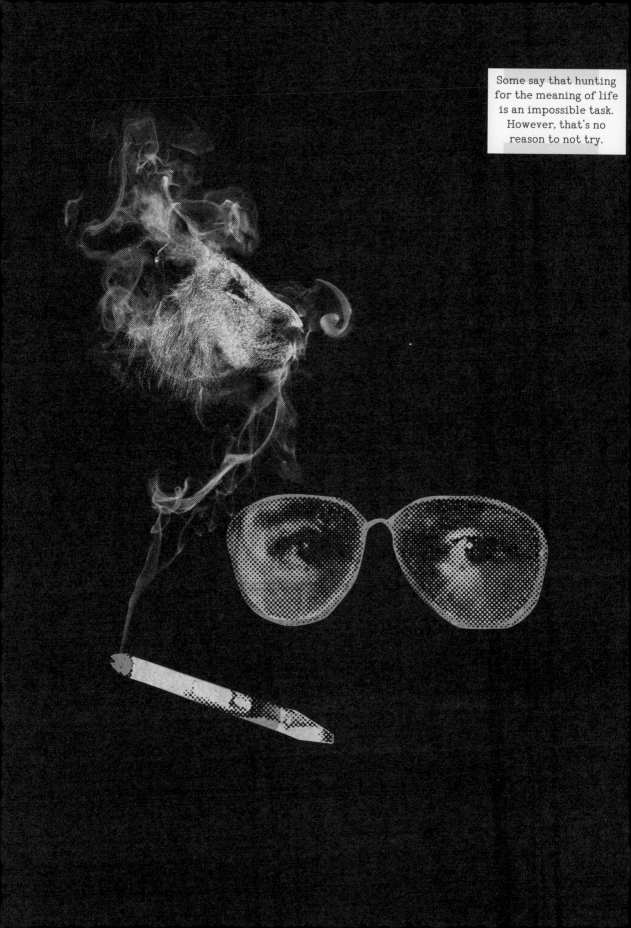

Some say that hunting for the meaning of life is an impossible task. However, that's no reason to not try.

THE FLOATING OR THE SWIMMING

ANYONE CAN GO BIG GAME HUNTING. YOU NEED NOT BE A 'PHILOSOPHER' TO THROW A SPEAR AT A BEAST LARGER AND STRONGER THAN YOURSELF. BY THINKING BIG AND APPLYING COLD BLOODED CRITICAL THINKING, ANYONE IS CAPABLE. HERE, AMERICAN JOURNALIST AND AUTHOR HUNTER S. THOMPSON TAKES ON THE KING OF THE JUNGLE.

In a letter written to his friend Hume Logan in 1958, twenty year old Hunter takes a stab at the meaning of life. He begins by turning to Shakespeare's Hamlet to put a stake in the ground: "To be, or not to be: that is the question: Whether 'tis nobler in the mind to suffer the slings and arrows of outrageous fortune, or to take arms against a sea of troubles..."

This IS indeed the question as Hunter sees it: "whether to float with the tide, or to swim for a goal. It is a choice we must all make consciously or unconsciously at one time in our lives. So few people understand this! Think of any decision you've ever made which had a bearing on your future: I may be wrong, but I don't see how it could have been anything but a choice however indirect — between the two things I've mentioned: the floating or the swimming."

Another author of note, Oscar Wilde, had similar thoughts on the matter, saying "The aim of life is self-development. To realize one's nature perfectly - that is what each of us is here for." Wilde also drew a distinction between living life to the fullest, and merely existing, saying "Life cannot be written, life can only be lived. To live is the rarest thing in the world. Most people exist, that's all."

The tragedy of life, as Hunter sees it, is "we seek to understand the goal and not the man." The problem with this approach is that our perception of the goal changes every day, as we grow older and change with the natural ebb and flow of life. "When you were young, let us say that you wanted to be a fireman. I feel reasonably safe in saying that you no longer want to be a fireman. Why? Because your perspective has changed. It's not the fireman who has changed, but you".

Another person who has had an immeasurable impact on popular culture is John Lennon. It appears that he too understood this deceivingly simple concept from a very young age, saying "When I was 5 years old, my mother always told me that happiness was the key to life. When I went to school, they asked me what I wanted to be when I grew up. I wrote down 'happy'. They told me I didn't understand the assignment, and I told them they didn't understand life."

So is this it? Is it a way of life that one should be tracking, as oppose to a tangible goal or achievement?

Hunter appears to believe so, saying it would be "foolish" to allow a goal, which one sees every day from a "different angle", mean we have to adjust our lives constantly. "How could we ever hope to accomplish anything other than galloping neurosis?"

But perhaps the quest for meaning is futile. The French philosopher Albert Camus said "You will never be happy if you continue to search for what happiness consists of. You will never live if you are looking for the meaning of life."

Never one to heed the advice of the wise, Hunter moves in for the kill, hurling his spear at this illusive beast with all his force: "As I see it then, the formula runs something like this: a man must choose a path which will let his ABILITIES function at maximum efficiency toward the gratification of his DESIRES. In doing this, he is fulfilling a need (giving himself identity by functioning in a set pattern toward a set goal) he avoids frustrating his potential (choosing a path which puts no limit on his self-development), and he avoids the terror of seeing his goal wilt or lose its charm as he draws closer to it (rather than bending himself to meet the demands of that which he seeks, he has bent his goal to conform to his own abilities and desires)."

Whatever you decide, whether life has meaning or not. Or if it's even possible to try and capture it, let's close on Hunter's final sage word of advice, "A man who procrastinates in his CHOOSING will inevitably have his choice made for him by circumstance".

So you can either float with the tide. Or swim in a direction of your choosing. ❖

THE TOWER OF KNOWLEDGE

Human beings are inquisitive creatures who are naturally curious about life and our place in the universe.

Philosophy is not only about getting the answers to the big questions, but is also about the process of using logic and reason to try and hunt down the answers.

It's said Socrates laid the foundations of Western philosophy by developing debate and argument as a technique. His student Plato built upon this platform to help construct a vision of a just society in *Republic*.

Plato was a profound influence on his student Aristotle, who despite disagreeing with his mentor on some fundamental points, continued building the tower of knowledge upwards.

Ever since, successive generations have climbed to the top, built upon (or torn down), and ultimately shone their own light out into the darkness, hoping to catch sight of the big game that roams these plains. ✤

REASON

ARISTOTLE

LOGIC

PLATO

REASON

SOCRATES

LOGIC

KNOWLEDGE

To catch the Killer Idea however,
requires a more creative approach
than standing still on a tower of
logic and reason built by others.
One must venture further into the
wild than the light of knowledge
can shine from any tower.

Thus, we must leave these
lands now and find our way
to the Black Lake of the
Subconscious Mind, if you're
to see for yourself where
ideas often spring from.

The big game hunter
strikes a light.
To break the darkness
of the night.

Toward the sound
of crunching bone.
Ventures into
the great unknown

And searches for tracks
that may yield a clue.
About the meaning of life
and knowledge that's true

JAMES WEBB YOUNG

PSYCHOLOGISTS FROM EARLY 20TH CENTURY

HUN

GATH

SIGMUND FREUD

J. P GUILFORD

TER

ERERS

FROM THE CONSCIOUS TO THE SUBCONSCIOUS

JAMES 'MEL' RHODES

GATHERING INSIGHTS ON IDEAS

Imagine if you will, that the mind is like a dense forest filled with high trees blocking out the daylight. Thoughts creep and crawl through the undergrowth, quietly hiding from sight.

The further in one goes, the darker it soon becomes. However, the hunter must push inward, gathering the sustenance and nutrition required for the creative journey. Thoughts are collected and examined. Their relationships and combinations scrutinized to discover which beasts may roam these parts.

Hidden in the middle of the forest, if one avoids becoming lost along the way, is the Black Lake of the Subconscious Mind.

If you stand in its shallows, you'll glimpse your reflection upon its surface. Don't be fooled. It is just that — a shimmering figment of the imagination — and has no real value or substance.

The hunter must wade out, plunge under and submerge deep, deep, down into its darkest depths, if one is to catch a glimpse of where a Killer Idea comes from.

By the early 20th century the subject of creativity was beginning to be studied and explored in greater depth by scientists and psychologists such as Graham Wallas, JP Guilford and James 'Mel' Rhodes.

Sigmund Freud shone a light on the significant yet little understood role which the subconscious has on influencing our thoughts and feelings. In 1939 American ad-exec James Webb Young eloquently articulated the idea generation process in a book titled *A Technique for Producing Ideas*.

This chapter combines their words of wisdom and pays tribute to their effort in gathering a healthy bundle of insights relating to the very nature of ideas - and creativity itself.

49

J.P. Guilford

GATHER & SORT

{DIVERGENT & CONVERGENT THINKING}

American psychologist J.P. Guilford is best remembered for his psychometric study of human intelligence, including the distinction between the divergent and convergent production of ideas. Here, we apply those principles to the gathering and sorting of information, that leads to creative problem solving.

PROBLEM

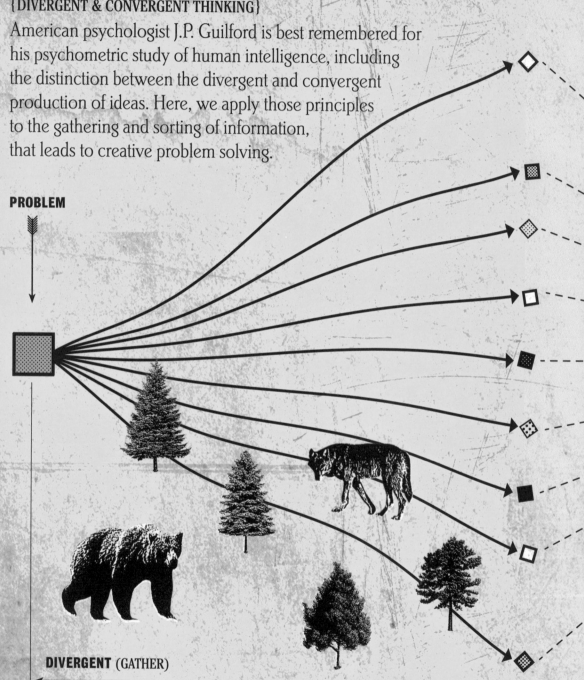

DIVERGENT (GATHER)

Divergent thinking happens in a spontaneous, free-flowing, 'non-linear' manner. Many ideas are gathered in an 'emergent cognitive fashion'. Multiple possible solutions are explored in a short amount of time, with unexpected connections being found.

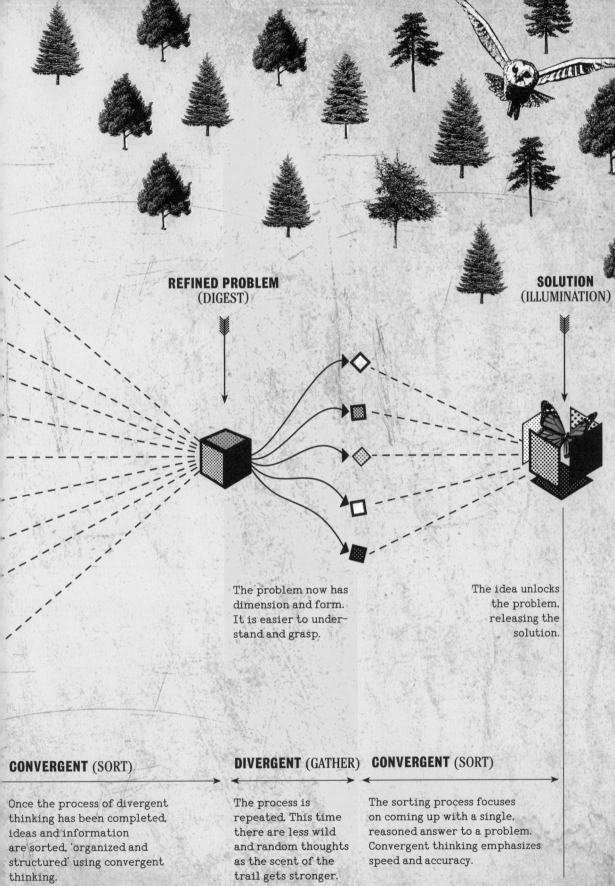

REFINED PROBLEM
(DIGEST)

SOLUTION
(ILLUMINATION)

The problem now has dimension and form. It is easier to understand and grasp.

The idea unlocks the problem, releasing the solution.

CONVERGENT (SORT)

Once the process of divergent thinking has been completed, ideas and information are sorted, 'organized and structured' using convergent thinking.

DIVERGENT (GATHER)

The process is repeated. This time there are less wild and random thoughts as the scent of the trail gets stronger.

CONVERGENT (SORT)

The sorting process focuses on coming up with a single, reasoned answer to a problem. Convergent thinking emphasizes speed and accuracy.

STEP 1. {GATHER}

GATHERING RAW MATERIAL

Over the following five spreads we pay homage to James Webb Young and his brilliant assessment of how ideas are produced.

Webb Young says the first step is to gather as much raw material as possible from your environment.

He describes two different types of information that need to be collected, referring to these as "the specific and the general."

Specific knowledge derives from the task at hand, such as product attributes and insights into the target audience.

By leaving no stone unturned, you ensure that as much information as possible is collected, so that it can be examined in closer detail at a later stage.

The second type of information is general knowledge. This requires much broader roaming, and is more a way of life, than a specific activity. A curious mind, is a sponge that absorbs all of the clues and stimuli that life provides. Often wandering off the beaten track, to explore less trodden paths.

By gathering a large quantity of facts and information, you'll have a good supply of food to consume. But of course, it isn't the belly that's being fed here, but the mind.

This stage of the process is similar to that which occurs within a kaleidoscope. "Every turn of its crank shifts the bits of glass into a new relationship and reveals a new pattern. The mathematical possibilities of such new combinations in the kaleidoscope are enormous, and the greater the number of pieces of glass in it the greater become the possibilities for new and striking combinations."

So too it is with the mind, the more raw material gathered, the greater the chances for creating new and original ideas. ➔

PLAY WITH YOUR FOOD

All quotes on this spread: *A Technique for Producing Ideas*. James Webb Young.

The information that has been gathered is allowed to float around the mind for a period of gestation. "What you do" says Webb Young "Is take the different bits of material, which you have gathered and feel them all over, as it were, with the tentacles of the mind".

During this phase, random combinations of specific and general knowledge are placed together to see if they connect or repel. What creates a friction or tension? Can sense be made out of disparate facts, as the mind searches for new relationships?

What the tentacles are trying to find is a "synthesis where everything will come together in a neat combination, like a jig-saw puzzle."

An important point, notes Webb Young, is that the mind tires in the same manner as the body does. But just like with the body, there is a second wind that comes. So his advice here is to keep trying, in the knowledge that a second wave of mental energy will arrive. ➤

TURN
OUT THE
LIGHTS

Once you've had a chance to fully digest all of the gathered material, "what you have to do at this time, apparently, is to turn the problem over to your unconscious mind and let it work while you sleep."

This may sound counter-intuitive, but Webb Young claims that once you've reached the third stage in the production of an idea, you have to "drop the problem completely and turn to whatever stimulates your imagination and emotion." Whittle a stick, read a book, go for a walk, or best of all, fall asleep.

From the outside looking in, it would appear that nothing is happening. But inside creatures are beginning to stir as the subconscious processing gets under way.

It is now that the hunter submerges into the Black Lake of the Subconscious Mind, searching to catch a glimpse of two or more thoughts combining "effectively to result in creative thinking." ➵

All quotes on this spread: *A Technique for Producing Ideas. James Webb Young.*

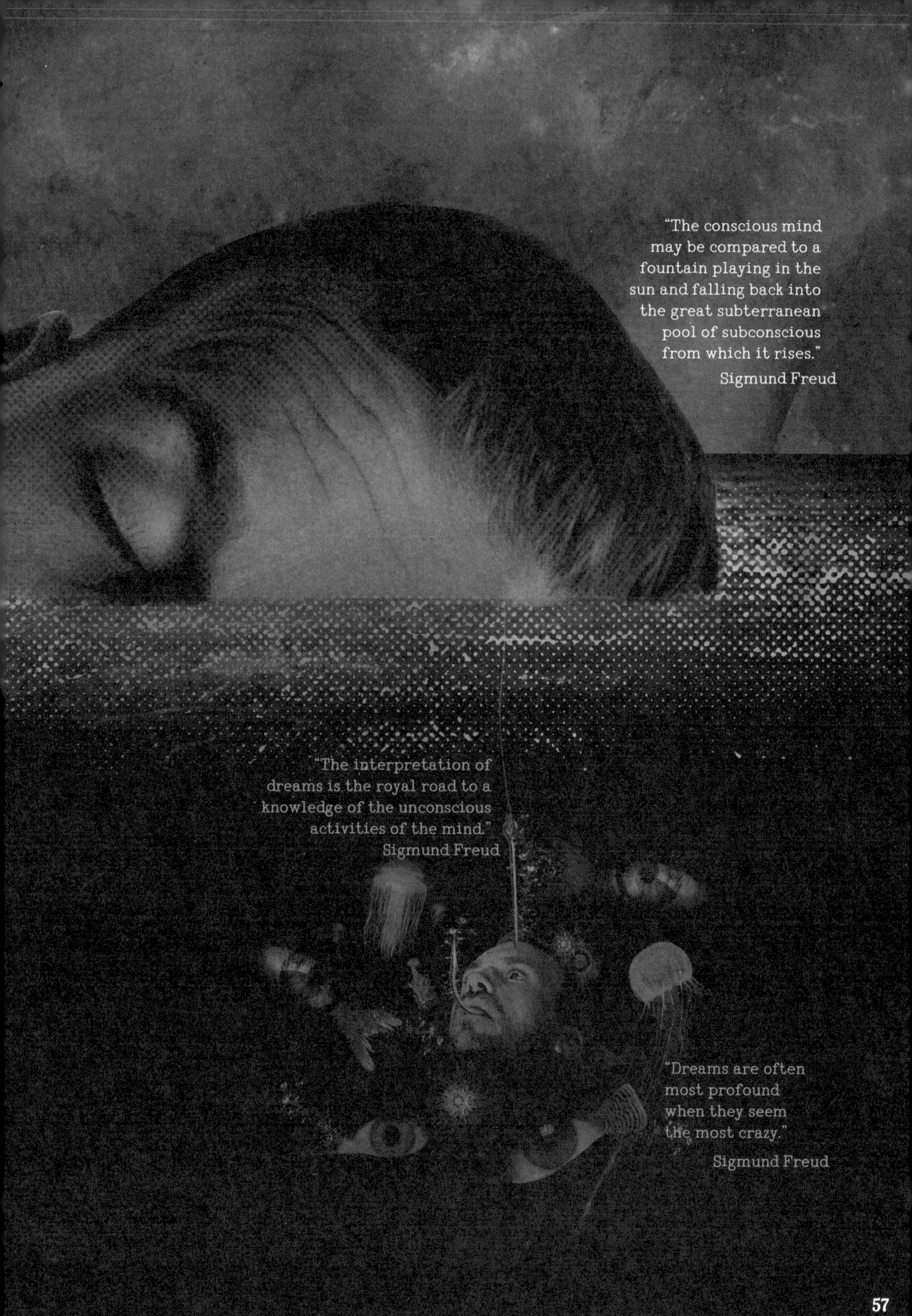

"The conscious mind may be compared to a fountain playing in the sun and falling back into the great subterranean pool of subconscious from which it rises."

Sigmund Freud

"The interpretation of dreams is the royal road to a knowledge of the unconscious activities of the mind."
Sigmund Freud

"Dreams are often most profound when they seem the most crazy."

Sigmund Freud

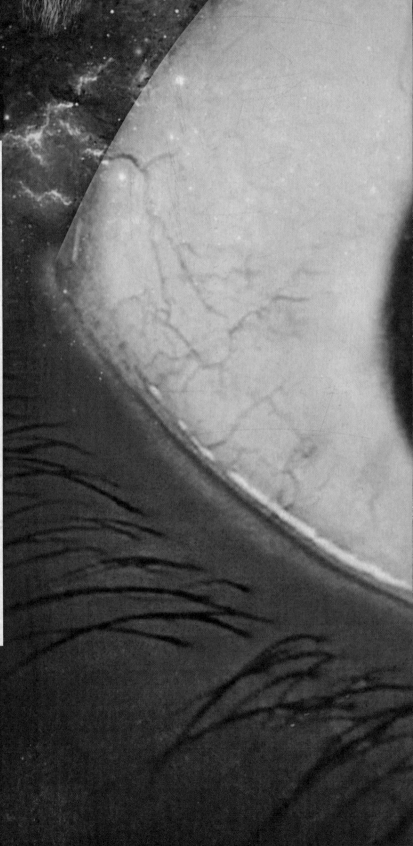

THE FLASH OF BRILLIANCE

The flash of brilliance occurs, only once all of the digested information has had a chance to incubate and float around. All of a sudden, something will "click into an illuminating new formation" says Webb Young. "Out of nowhere the Idea will appear. It will come to you when you are least expecting it."

This brilliant burst of light, is something "that the conscious self can't will and the subliminal self can only welcome" as a successful train of association locks into place.

This newly formed, successful idea "has probably been preceded by a series of tentative and unsuccessful trains. The series of unsuccessful trains of association may last for periods varying, from a few seconds to several hours. Sometimes the successful train seems to consist of a single leap of association, or of successive leaps which are so rapid as to be almost instantaneous." The effect may fool us into thinking that ideas just simply happen, without the preceding steps taking place. ➨

All quotes on this spread: *A Technique for Producing Ideas.* James Webb Young.

58

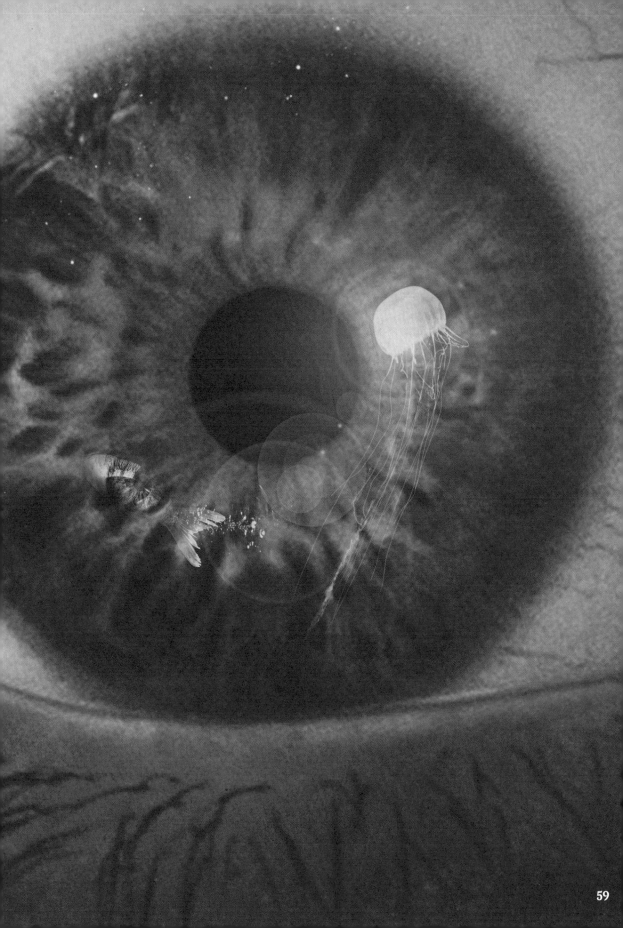

STEP 5. {BIRTH}

THE MOMENT OF TRUTH

The moment of truth arrives, when the new idea has to be delivered into the real world. Webb Young notes that at this point, you usually discover that your child is not quite as "brilliant" as it seemed, when it was first given birth to.

"Do not make the mistake, of holding your idea close to your chest at this stage. Submit it to the criticism of the judicious.

When you do, a surprising thing will happen. You will find that a good idea has, as it were, self expanding qualities. It stimulates those who see it, to add to it. Thus possibilities in it, which you have overlooked, will come to light."

It may need to be defended and nurtured for some time, but if your idea can find its feet, it has a chance of not only surviving, but contributing to the world.

IN SUMMARY

James Webb Young's *A Technique for Producing Ideas* has stood the test of time since its original publication in 1939. There are two principles he suggests are worthwhile remembering.

Two general principles regarding the producing of new ideas.

1. An idea is nothing more nor less than the combination of old elements.

2. The capacity to bring old elements into new combinations depends largely on the ability to see new relationships.

"To some minds each fact is a separate piece of knowledge. To others it is a link in a chain of knowledge. It has relationships and similarities. It is not so much a fact as it is an illustration of a general law applying to a whole series of facts. To a mind which is quick to see relationships several ideas will occur. Consequently the habit of mind which leads to a search for relationships between facts becomes of the highest importance in the production of ideas." ✤

All quotes on this spread: *A Technique for Producing Ideas*. James Webb Young.

Come my friend, we've spent
enough time here. 'Tis time
to see what new challenges
await us on our journey.

In the forest
where creatures creep.
Is a lake
that's black and deep.

Close your eyes
and open your mind.
Subconscious treasures
you will find.

Just hold your breath
and dive deep down.
Pluck a jewel
from the crown.

CULTURE • RESOURCES • HABITAT

MOU
GUI

ATTITIUDE · KNOWLEDGE · IMAGINATION

THE HARD SLOG

The creative endeavour is notorious for its difficulties and challenges. Unfortunately the Killer Idea is more often than not found on the far side of this rocky range.

Seasoned hunters will tell you that in every journey, you'll reach a point where further progress simply feels impossible. That a mountain of work needs to be overcome before any headway is likely to be made.

But much like climbing to the summit, if prepared and committed, the only reason a mountain can't be conquered, is if it's believed it can't be climbed.

To help us get over this obstacle are two experienced mountain guides.

Edward de Bono has been plotting paths for well over 50 years, often finding unexpected tracks which weren't previously known.

Professor Tina Seelig guides not only a way over but also shows how to fuel the body and soul, to ensure one doesn't run out of puff, stuck half way up on an icy ledge.

VERTICAL THINKING (LOGIC)

Mountain Guide: Edward de Bono

Lateral thinking is a term coined by Edward de Bono and is a method used to solve problems through an indirect and creative approach. "It differs from 'vertical' thinking in that it doesn't rely on a chain of logic to arrive at an answer." De Bono claims it is a more useful method than "horizontal" imagination in that the lateral approach is concerned with "the detailed implementation of an idea, rather than just having a multitude of random thoughts."

Whilst "vertical" logic often yields a high probability of results, the dynamic qualities of "lateral thinking are advantageous for prevailing in a changing and chaotic world."

In the same way a hunter can learn the terrain by closely studying a map, it is getting out, walking around and viewing an environment from all its different angles that gives an enriched understanding of the task at hand.

THE CORE PRINCIPLES OF LATERAL THINKING

THINKING

LATERAL

HORIZONTAL THINKING (IMAGINATIVE)

1.

RECOGNITION OF DOMINANT POLARISING IDEAS

Dominant ideas have a powerful effect, as they frame thinking in a way that acknowledges the idea's influence, even if it isn't apparent. "Old and adequate ideas, like old and adequate cities, come to polarise everything around them. All organisation is based on them. Minor alterations can be made to the outskirts, but it is impossible to change the whole structure radically."

Dominant ideas polarise, as they create 'conventional wisdom', which the majority adopts as gospel, whilst those seeking progress will rebel against.

Climbing tip: To escape the influence of dominant ideas, deliberately write down and define the factors that appear to be dominating the situation.

2.

THE SEARCH FOR DIFFERENT WAYS OF LOOKING AT THINGS

It is the ability to look at existing problems from different angles that has always been a hallmark of human progress. Finding new perspectives allows you to better evaluate what the value of something is, for example "you can look at monarchy as antiquated and expensive, or as a system which averts a more dangerous selection for the head of state."

The purpose of the search is to find as many different ways over the mountain as possible. Once a variety of pathways have been discovered, you can then evaluate which way will be most suitable.

Climbing tip: A good way to start looking at things differently is to hunt for any underlying relationships, connections or patterns.

3.

RELAXATION OF THE RIGID CONTROL OF VERTICAL THINKING

A rigid dependance on the security that logic provides, becomes an inhibiting factor during the creative process. "There is an extreme type of temperament which compulsively seeks for tight control of what goes on in the mind... a striving for a meticulousness and precision which is as artificial as a strip of film reel which divides motion up into a series of static images."

As it is only the final conclusion that must be correct, lateral thinking "happily takes you off the beaten path."

Climbing tip: The best way to relax the rigid control of vertical thinking is to embrace the chaos of the creativity - safe in the knowledge that many great inventions have arisen through a process of trial and error.

4.

THE USE OF CHANCE

The purpose of chance in the creative process is to help you to look at things differently, and to also disrupt thinking which gets you stuck in a rut.

The beauty of random associations is that they "can generate unexpected and surprising solutions."

Climbing tip: One way to stimulate creativity is to randomly select an object from somewhere in your environment. A pencil, pot plant or even a word out of a dictionary. Then try to associate it with the area you are working with, to coax out random thoughts.

All quotes on this spread: 'Lateral Thinking'. By Edward de Bono.

TOOLS & TECHNIQUES

When attempting to conquer the creative mountain, lateral thinking offers a selection of tools which can help smash restricting thought patterns or help out if you're stuck in a rut. According to Edward de Bono, the mind is a pattern making system. The basis of its effectiveness is that it creates patterns out of information so that it may be more easily recognised and understood when next encountered. This selection of tools are designed to help rearrange the available information so as to aid in the problem solving process.

GENERATE ALTERNATIVES

Edward de Bono says that it is a common trap to not look beyond the obvious for alternative solutions. Stating that "generating alternative concepts creates a breeding ground for new ideas, so the purpose is to loosen up rigid ways of looking at things.

A good way to start the lateral thinking process is to describe the "problem or situation in as many different ways as possible." As the purpose of creativity is to either solve a problem, progress forward or evolve the existing mind-set.

What you're trying to capture are the "differences, similarities, relationships, complexities, simplicity or significance".

One way to stimulate this process is to set a fixed quota of alternatives that must be achieved before you can move on to the next challenge.

SHIFT FOCUS

By shifting focus, one is able to climb the mountain more effectively. Either study the immediate rockface to discover the finer details. Or gaze up, to gain the bigger picture of where it is you're heading and how you're going to get there.

The following spread shows how you can shift focus by using "parallel thinking".

PROVOKE

When we provoke someone, we're essentially trying to see what they're made of. Testing their mettle to determine the underlying substance. The same is true with provoking an idea. We are deliberately trying to make the situation 'pop' to see if it's only hot air inside or if there's something surprising hidden within.

"New ideas can be stimulated by using provocative thinking techniques such as —wishful thinking, exaggeration, reversal, escapism, distortion, metaphor or analogy".

SUSPEND JUDGEMENT

De Bono notes that the embarrassment associated with being wrong is a very real barrier to creating new ideas. The "inhibiting fear" of making mistakes is counter-productive to the objective of creating multiple ideas.

"The suspension of judgement can allow an idea to survive longer and will breed further ideas. Ideas can be accepted for their stimulating effect instead of being rejected.

Ideas which are judged wrong within the current frame of reference may even survive long enough to show that the frame of reference needs rethinking."

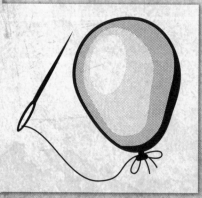

"TWO UNIT DIVISION"

The use of a two-unit division system can be employed to generate a range of information relating to the subject.

For example, if you were asked to devise a mountain climbing system one could divide the problem into bite size chunks.

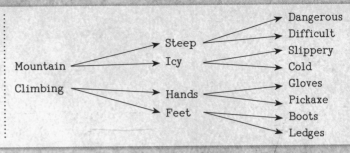

WARM UP EXERCISES

To avoid injury, try using lateral thinking to solve the following puzzels. (Answers at base).

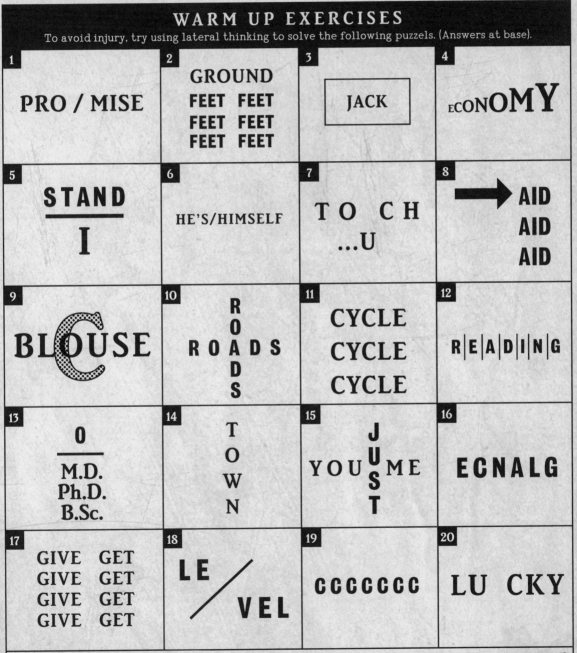

1 PRO / MISE

2 GROUND
FEET FEET
FEET FEET
FEET FEET

3 JACK

4 ᴇᴄᴏɴ**OMY**

5 STAND / I

6 HE'S/HIMSELF

7 TO CH ...U

8 → AID AID AID

9 BL**C**OUSE

10 ROADS (ROADS)

11 CYCLE CYCLE CYCLE

12 R|E|A|D|I|N|G

13 O / M.D. Ph.D. B.Sc.

14 TOWN (vertical)

15 YOU **JUST** ME

16 ECNALG

17 GIVE GET / GIVE GET / GIVE GET / GIVE GET

18 LE / VEL

19 CCCCCCC

20 LU CKY

PARALLEL THINKING

Parallel thinking is a technique devised by Edward de Bono in 1985 whereby a group of hunters work in unison to capture the prey.

It is an effective and time efficient method of cooperative exploration, where as much relevant information, opinions and hunches relating to the subject in question are collected.

To fully understand a problem, requires looking at it from all available angles.

Parallel thinking provides a framework in which everyone approaches the problem from the "same angle at the same moment".

This technique is recommended when the hunting party is required to cover as much ground as possible.

The direction of thinking is indicated by six coloured hats, each of which offers a different mode of thinking:

BLUE HAT
OVERVIEW

The blue hat is like the conductor of the orchestra. Sets the sequence of discussion, defines the focus, is in charge of the summary and lays out 'next steps'.

AGENDA / DECISION / GLOBAL OVERVIEW

ASK:

- What is the subject?
- What are we thinking about?
- What is the goal?

GREEN HAT
CREATIVITY

The green hat asks for ideas, alternatives, possibilities and designs.

IMAGINATION / PROVOCATION / INVESTIGATION

ASK:

- What if?
- What might?
- Why not?

WHITE HAT
INFORMATION

Considering purely what information is available, what are the facts? (From hard facts to soft information such as rumours and personal experience).

FACT / DATA / FIGURES

ASK:

- What do we know?
- What do we need to know?
- What is missing?
- What questions should we ask?
- How might we get the information we need?

RED HAT
EMOTIONS

The red hat allows intuitive or instinctive gut reactions or statements of emotional feeling.

EMOTIONS / HUNCHES / FEELINGS / INSTINCTS

SAY:

- I don't like this because...
- My gut feeling is...
- My intuition is telling me...

OPTIMISM
HAT: YELLOW

The yellow hat is used to look for the obvious and hidden benefits to a proposal. The intention is to find value and why something should work.

VALUE / BENEFITS / PROS

ASK:

- What is the value?
- Can we find more hidden value?
- What are the benefits?

BLACK HAT
CAUTION

The black hat is the basis for critical thinking and is used for risk assessment.

CRITICAL / ANALYTICAL / DISCERNING

ASK:

- Does this fit our values?
- Does this fit our strategic objective?
- Does this fit our abilities?
- Does this fit our resources?

INFORMATION

OPTIMISM

OVERVIEW

CREATIVITY

CAUTION

EMOTION

THE INNOVATION ENGINE

Tina Seelig likens creativity to gymnastics, noting that it is "quite complex and is influenced by many factors, such as your knowledge, motivation and environment. It makes sense to consider all the variables that influence ingenuity and how they all fit together."

Seelig developed the 'innovation engine' as a model to help maximise the power of your inner engine by learning how to draw strength from the outer world.

THE INNER ENGINE:

There are three interlinked parts to your inner engine. They are your attitude, knowledge and imagination.

"YOUR ATTITUDE sparks your curiosity to acquire knowledge, and sets the innovation engine in motion.

YOUR KNOWLEDGE provides the fuel for your imagination, allowing you to generate innovative ideas.

YOUR IMAGINATION is the catalyst for the transformation of knowledge into new ideas."

CUL

ATTITUD

IMAG

HABITAT

All quotes on this spread: 'Ingenius. A Crash Course on Creativity'. By Tina Seelig.

"IT ISN'T THE MOUNTAIN AHEAD THAT WEARS YOU OUT; IT'S THE GRAIN OF SAND IN YOUR SHOE."

ROBERT W. SERVICE

RE

KNOWLEDGE

RESOURCES

THE OUTER ENGINE:

The inner process of transforming attitude, knowledge and imagination into a creative application are influenced by a myriad of factors. The three most important factors on the outside of your innovation engine are:

"RESOURCES are all the assets in your community.

HABITATS are the local environments, including your home, school or office.

CULTURE is the collective beliefs, values and behaviours in your community.

These environmental factors can either stimulate or inhibit your creativity."

HOW THE INNOVATION ENGINE WORKS:

INNER ← TRANSFORMS → OUTER

All quotes on this spread: Ingenius: A Crash Course on Creativity'. By Tina Seelig.

ATTITUDE

"Your attitude is the spark which jump starts your creativity. Without the attitude that you can come up with breakthrough ideas, your innovation engine will never get going. Your mindset determines how you interpret and respond to situations and whether you are driven to go out and gain knowledge or not."

Every single person contributes to the culture in which they live. As individuals we contribute to our family, school and any other organisations we may be part of. So culture is effectively the collective attitudes of those who live there.

CULTURE

"Culture refers to the ways in which groups of people perceive, interpret and understand the world around them. We are all extremely sensitive to our culture - from the moment we wake up we are immersed in a cultural stew that deeply influences our thoughts and actions."

KNOWLEDGE

"Your knowledge fuels your imagination, allowing you to generate innovative ideas.

The more you know about a particular topic, the more raw materials you have to work with to generate ideas.

Serial entrepreneurs who start companies in diverse fields, are masters at building on their accumulated knowledge from past ventures."

The more knowledge you gain, the more able you are to utilise it. For example "the more you know about fishing, the more fish you catch. The more fish you catch, the greater knowledge of fishing you have."

RESOURCES

"Resources are all the things of value in your environment. They come in all different forms, including natural resources such as individuals with expertise in a subject who can act as guides and organisations such as universities or local firms that foster innovation. Also, information resources such as libraries and the internet."

IMAGINATION

"Your imagination - the ability to create something new - is a powerful force. It is the catalyst required for creative combustion. Without it, new ideas are impossible to generate.

Broad knowledge of an array of different subjects is an important way of ensuring the imagination always has plenty of material to work with."

Cafés and bars provide a good example of this correlation. A zany café with quirky decor is likely to stimulate more offbeat conversation. Whilst a Sports bar encourages a different range of subjects to be discussed. The environment provides stimulation and sets the tone.

HABITAT

"The habitats we create are essentially external manifestations of our imagination. We create physical spaces that reflect the way we think, and in turn, those habitats influence our imagination. Managers, teachers, parents and community leaders play an important role in creating habitats which foster imagination in their employees, students and children."

"IMAGINATION: THE CATALYST REQUIRED FOR CREATIVE COMBUSTION. WITHOUT IT, NEW IDEAS ARE IMPOSSIBLE TO GENERATE."
TINA SEELIG

CHANGE THE FRAME

The way we look at the world directly impacts on our ability to solve problems.

Seelig says that "mastering the ability to reframe problems is an important tool for increasing your imagination, because it unlocks a vast array of solutions."

Reframing problems isn't easy, but the benefit is that it allows you to "see the world in a brand new light". A great way to begin generating "imaginative responses to the problems that come your way" is to ask questions that start with "Why." This will help you to see the world from others' perspectives and reframe your own perspective.

"What is the sum of 5 plus 5?" What two numbers add up to 10?" The first question has only one right answer, and the second has an infinite number of solutions, including negative numbers and fractions. These two questions differ only in the way they are framed".

By reframing a problem, it's possible to dramatically increase the range of available solutions.

CROSS-POLLINATE

PLACES

PEOPLE

CONNECT AND COMBINE RANDOM ASSOCIATIONS.

OBJECTS

IDEAS

The cross-pollination of ideas and opinions are essential for innovative progress. By randomly connecting places, existing ideas and objects - it is possible to discover relationships that will spark new ideas.

"Communities that are at the crossroads of the world such as ancient Alexandria and Istanbul or modern Hong Kong, London and New York, which attract people from vastly different cultures, benefit from the cross-pollination of ideas and increased creativity."

All quotes on this spread: 'Ingenius. A Crash Course on Creativity'. By Tina Seelig.

Seelig cites numerous examples of how either the geographic location, concentration, or proximity to others has had a positive effect on the creative output.

"Silicon Valley innovation is robust because of the extensive cross-pollination of ideas between individuals and companies. Firms are concentrated in a small area, which leads to more informal interactions and easier formal connections".

Civic spaces are intentionally built into town planning to encourage people from all different walks of life to come together and rub shoulders. The result is that random people, with random thoughts and ideas are provided with a space where they can cross-pollinate intentionally or unintentionally.

"The more diverse the inputs, the more interesting and innovative the outputs. For instance, places in the world that have a large influx of immigrants end up with fascinating food fusions. A good example is Lima, Peru, where a new cuisine has emerged from mixing of local Latin American ingredients and traditional Spanish dishes with a strong influence from the cuisines of China, Italy, Africa and Japan.

Steve Jobs said that what made the original Macintosh computer so great was that the people working on it were "musicians and poets, and artists and zoologists, and historians, who also happened to be the best computer scientists in the world." Apple took inspiration from their knowledge of these diverse fields to create something that was completely novel."

Looks like we've almost made it over the mountain. Time now to see what inspriration can be found on the other side.

If the challenge
of the climb ahead.
And its peril
fills the heart with dread.

Fear not the heights
that you must scale.
And certainly not
that you may fail.

Put one foot first
and then the other.
Inner strength
you'll soon discover.

CULTU

CAT

HUNTING INSPIRATION

The most powerful art always has a certain raw quality to it. An honesty, authenticity and realness which connects at a deep emotional level.

It will say something about the world we live in, our place in the universe and the culture which shapes us.

To capture these things, the hunter must not only confront the inner turmoil of the soul, but also explore where it has come from and what has created it in the first place.

To do so, the artist must sit patiently and observe the world which swirls around their head.

After a period of introspection, the hunter looks outward at society, trying to catch a glimpse as it were, at the intangible nature of culture. Morals, beliefs, customs, attitudes, values, style and aesthetics all fly around together.

They form a swarm, creating a discernable shape and body which appears to have a mind of its own.

Now, the artist releases their soul to fly amongst the cultural cloud, hunting for anything which catches the eye and will provide the necessary inspiration.

In these pages we pull
together the thoughts of
a musician, graffiti artist,
poet, photographer and other
hunters who only know it's
right, when it feels right.
Yes they have skill and ability,
but it is intuition and gut
instinct which sets them apart.

LIAM HOWLETT
THE PRODIGY. LONDON, U.K.

CLOSE TO INSANITY

How does it begin?

It starts off by us all getting together and talking about what kind of record we want to make, what we liked about the last album, what do we want to make and carry over from that. Anyone got any ideas, usually none of us have any ideas, you know what I mean, but we all wanna do it. Each album is different, for example on this album, we went into studio and started from scratch. What used to happen is I'd have 5 or 6 instrumentals ready to go and the guys would come in at that stage and I'd have a rough idea.

What's the creative process?

It's a real process, goes through different stages. I'm on the road all the time, but I try to catch time after a show and put little ideas on the laptop, to ignite energy later on. 30 sec bit of an idea, loops, or a melody, or something. I tend to go through various stages of pretty close to insanity with the writing process, I drive myself quite mad, it's not easy. I don't do it on purpose it just has to get to this stage. If an idea doesn't work straight away, it doesn't feel like its gonna work, then put it on the shelf. I've learnt a good idea will always be a good idea. If you come back to that it still feels half decent, a month or two later, it's got

something about it that's good. I record everything, it's always best to get it down, and then listen to it. As I've gone on, 20 yrs, 24 yrs down the line, still learning about myself with the creative process. There's no rule I can stick to. With this record I'd rinsed myself totally with first 8 or 9 months of studio in day time. I had to up the intensity somehow so started working at night, and you're in a different head space. Like I'm very difficult to live with during this stage. I've got a wife and kid and try to be a good husband and father, but it's really hard to do simple things like go to dinner, my head's not there, Once in the zone, I'm there, it's hard to be knocked off.

More recently, on the last couple of albums, the way I write songs, I rarely write songs in one go. I'll write 50% of it, then stick it on the shelf for maybe even a month, then work on something else. I've 2-3 ideas working at same time so it doesn't get boring. My attention span is quite short. I have to keep myself excited, so I'll hit it hard to begin with then I like to leave it for a bit and if it's any good will still sound alright in a couple of weeks time. It's a funny thing man. Don't know rules of how I best operate. It's a real mind fuck. The nature of the music industry and way shit is now, it's like fast food, kids digest it so quickly. Going back 10 years, albums would last 1 ½ years, can stretch singles out. Albums last just over half a year - so rapid fire. I'm already thinking about the next thing. Good in a way, you move on.

Where do you get inspiration?

The creative mind you have to feed it. You can't expect a mind to be the same brain you had 15 years ago. Got to keep shit fresh and keep inspiration flowing in.

When I had the studio in West London, I used to just walk down Portobello road and just soak up the shit. My ears are always open, it's happened a few times while out for dinner with the Mrs, sitting in a Lebanese or Egyptian restaurant and heard their mad music on the sound system and I've gone up and asked them about it and I've ended up sampling it. The point is inspiration can strike at any point. Things can hit you. You can be anywhere, just have to be ready to capture it. The dictaphone on my phone gets so much use. My brain can't remember all the stuff I want to remember. I love that. As I've got older, I've learnt inspiration can literally come from anything. Could be in a down time when I don't feel particularly inspired. Like tomorrow in Moscow, I know for sure, when I step foot outside, go onto the street I know I'll see and hear something that will make me go, oh shit!

What's your your Killer Idea?

The moment I thought I wanna do this was when I heard a record from Grand Master Flash and it was made of other people's music mixed together. That was my in, I thought I can do this. That was that. It wasn't until I met the others that things aligned - the rave culture in the UK, suddenly everything made sense, when I started writing that music, I knew I'd found my home. It included all my influences from Hip Hop. If there's any music I was meant to write, this was it. That was when I knew, this is me. I gave up my job and threw myself into it. ✤

Interview:

MARINA MUUN
ILLUSTRATOR: LONDON, UK.

GOOD THINGS COME TO THE SURFACE

Where have you come from, where are you now?

I'm from Varna, Bulgaria originally. I moved to England 7 years ago and now live and work in London.

What's been the biggest challenge on your journey?

Being able to make a living from something that I love and enjoy doing. I feel very lucky to get up in the morning and make images which will make other people happy and make the world a bit more colourful. But I'm at the very start of my career and I believe you need to challenge yourself daily in order to grow as an artist and as a person. Take on different projects and don't get too comfortable.

Describe your style?

Style is important and necessary as illustration is a commercial art but it's only part of the equation. When I start working on an image I never start out by concentrating on the style. Instead, I always try to get a good solid idea first which communicates the concept at hand. Illustration is a product - it has to look good but it also has to function. Ideas come first, style is secondary. Styles go out of fashion and focusing on a style can be really restrictive - being a good visual thinker is more valuable.

What inspires you?

I collect images of all kinds of things - photography, ceramics, book covers, fine art, graphic design, woodblock prints, everything really. It's so important to keep feeding your mind new things. I also sometimes listen to documentaries on artists lives while working - recently I listened to one on Magritte.

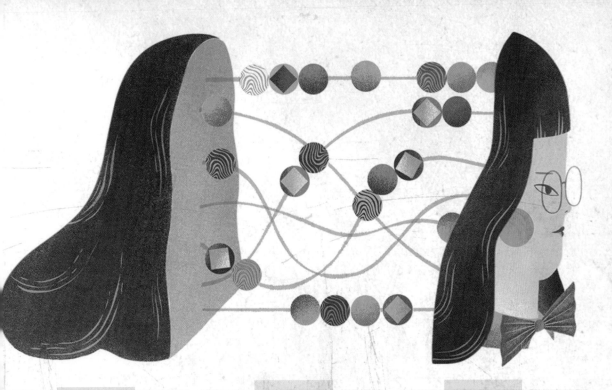

Describe your creative process?

My creative process is largely determined by time and whether I'm working to a brief or something personal. Deadlines can be really tight so I mostly make my illustrations digitally. I start out by reading the brief a few times and jotting down some key ideas and phrases which serve as focus points when I later try to come up with some visual solutions. Sometimes I only start sketching a day or two after I've read the brief. I feel like my brain has more time to process the ideas and for some good things to come to the surface. This is in a way the most challenging process because the concept is the backbone of the illustration. When I have my concept I will scan my sketch and work on it in Photoshop.

What happens if you get stuck?

I'm usually working on a few different things so if I get a bit stuck or tired while working on one piece I switch to something else and give my brain some time to do some more processing in the background. I go for a walk, meet up with a friend for a coffee and sit at the desk with a fresh mind and renewed energy.

Best advice received?

Work hard and be nice to people. ❖

MATT McATEER

POET: CHESTERFIELD, U.K.

SOMETHING
HUMAN

How'd you get into poetry?

I've always scribbled ideas down, a bit of writing. I started writing a book initially. A couple of characters I used, one was an aspiring stand up comedian. I'd written a set for him. I started going to comedy clubs, thought I'd give it a go. I was writing more and more poetry, by chance came across a night in Sheffield that did it, and started going to that and it sort of went from there.

What are you writing about?

A lot of it is about work culture. Films in the 90s. About looking back to the 80s. About coal mines shutting down, and what the industry is going through, where I live. Sort of being replaced by more transient temporary jobs and a lot of instability. One of the characters gets all sorts of psychological problems, drink problems. Another one reacts to it by being involved in petty crime. So, that gives you a lot of scope to explore loads of different things.

I use all sorts of pop culture references, so some song lyrics might be really cheesy, some that some people might perceive as being more cool. New York Dolls quotes, next to cheesy ones. Even really trashy television programmes. If you put telly on and get a little bit of info about a show, one from Geordie Shore, The Only Way is Essex. Really trashy telly. And then put that next to a paraphrasing from Dickens. It doesn't really matter if it's high or low, it's flooding everywhere in a blur. It's difficult to separate what might be worth your attention, or not worth your attention, as we are just bombarded with images all the time.

I'm trying to find something human. I tend to write characters rather than first person. I don't want to be too lecturing. I'd rather boil it down to a story and see what it means.

What do you mean when you say 'I believe in nothing'?

'I believe in nothing' came from the idea in an Adam Curtis documentary, Bitter Lake, about the situation in the Middle East. How the West doesn't seek to understand some of the cultures in the Middle East. He uses a phrase like 'politicians believe in nothing'. There's an emptiness in culture to some degree. With a lot of the politicians in the UK, it's an emptiness really, not a lot to believe in. The Labour leadership at the moment, until Jeremy Corbyn came and stood like a human being, the other three were completely interchangeable. Been to a politician school where you just talk crap.

Tell me about performing?

It's instant if you perform, if you write in a book, you don't know what reaction you are going to get, In performance you get that instantly. I like the craic. I like performing.

It's an oral tradition anyway, poetry. Goes back centuries. If you think of the great poets, Shakespeare, Christopher Munroe who wrote poetry in plays really. There to be performed . I think it would sound ridiculous to them for poetry not to be performed.

VOMIT SPUNK AND BL

WHAT MATERIALS

GRITTY AN PROVOCATIV

ADVI!

IRONY, ENIGMA SEEK P

THE VINE THAT THE PRIZE

WILL ALWAYS CROWNE

HEADS CAN ROLL

SYMBOL OF REVOLUTION

IN COUNTLESS NATION

BUT YOUR INSURGONT

IS LACKING DISTINCT

YOU'RE A PROBLEM CH

BOFRWOD OF RITA

RUNNING WILD

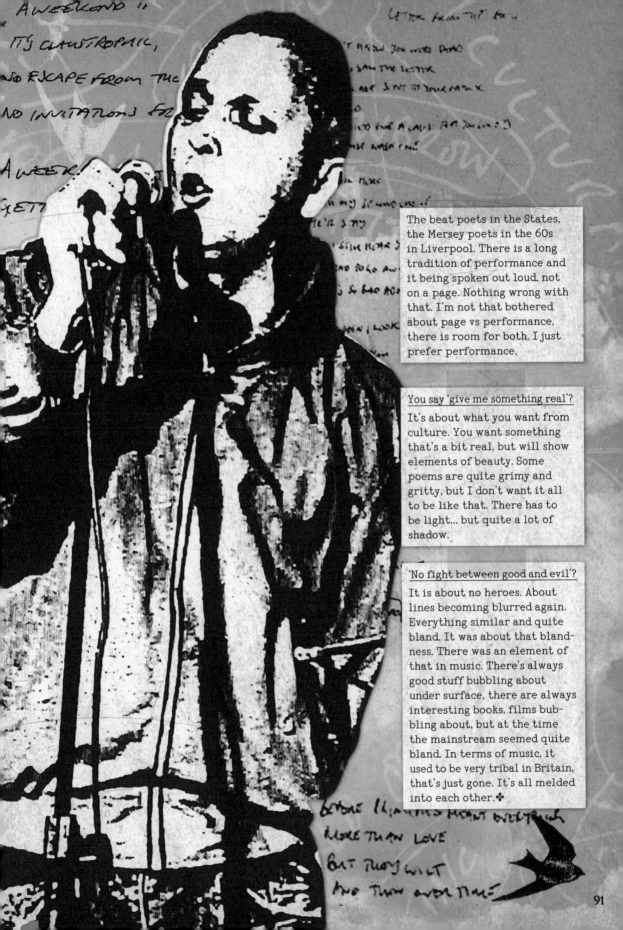

The beat poets in the States, the Mersey poets in the 60s in Liverpool. There is a long tradition of performance and it being spoken out loud, not on a page. Nothing wrong with that. I'm not that bothered about page vs performance, there is room for both. I just prefer performance.

You say 'give me something real'?

It's about what you want from culture. You want something that's a bit real, but will show elements of beauty. Some poems are quite grimy and gritty, but I don't want it all to be like that. There has to be light... but quite a lot of shadow.

'No fight between good and evil'?

It is about no heroes. About lines becoming blurred again. Everything similar and quite bland. It was about that blandness. There was an element of that in music. There's always good stuff bubbling about under surface, there are always interesting books, films bubbling about, but at the time the mainstream seemed quite bland. In terms of music, it used to be very tribal in Britain, that's just gone. It's all melded into each other. ❖

ASKEW ONE

GRAFFITI ARTIST: AUCKLAND, NEW ZEALAND.

SEE THINGS
THROUGH

What's the path been?

Where do I start? I came up painting graffiti, so firstly I was a graffiti writer. My art school was really the street and painting graffiti in its more traditional form and it was very letter based. Probably the last four to maybe six years I have diversified a lot in what I paint and how much my studio process informs my outdoor process, back and forth; it is more like a kind of conversation.

How did you find your style?

It came as a reaction to being in the graffiti scene where a lot of stylistic kind of stuff just gets recycled, e.g. it is very nostalgic and there is not a lot of innovation anymore in that realm, there is a lot of people painting almost a homage to the 70's and 80's New York graffiti and that just goes in cycles and I don't really feel that interested in that any more. When I stepped away from being as active in graffiti as I once was and started working on painting, I had completely forgotten how to paint anything but graffiti and I definitely went through a two year period of just experimenting with anything and everything until I finally stumbled over what I wanted to do and then set my mind to working at it. I believe that really good original stuff is the sum of all lessons learned applied so if you take all of that wealth of experience that you have had individually on your road, your path and then apply it to something, you are going to come up with something that is much more distinctly your own.

What keeps you going?

I am constantly making and experimenting and researching all at the same time so I could be painting a body of work and that is a finalised body that I am working towards for some end result like a show but then I usually have about three or four experimental pieces of work just laying around in the studio that I am also mucking around with. With no real strategy for them, I am just experimenting and I am always listening to podcasts, reading books, constantly keeping mindful of what is going on in the areas that I am interested in, to perculate those ideas for the next body. I am a pretty restless person and I don't do a lot of sitting still.

What's the role of art?

What I see arts job as being is just one of many ways of communicating powerful ideas and speaking about the kind of world that we live in. There's a weird attitude that it is wrong for people to speak up and go against the grain or speak up about injustices; there is an attitude that it's not appropriate or we shouldn't do that; since when? All of the greatest artists have always observed injustice and spoken about it. And it is only now that we live in this world once again where art is becoming something only for a very small minority of people at the top of the food chain. A lot of artists are pandering to that and are making work that is so vacuous and devoid of any kind of questioning or personality and I think that is a real shame because they are so wary of biting the hand that feeds. I really don't care who I upset. As long as I am not being an arsehole.

Best advice ever received?

You have to have your eyes open. I think the best bit of advice I try to give to people is about the power in "doing". It is really easy right at the beginning of your journey to be deterred really easily when things don't match your expectation; this becomes a really stifling energy. The way people succeed creatively in going to the next level is just by constantly doing, doing, doing and seeing things through. I think about the amount of half finished art works I have had because I was really discouraged by it not looking like the way it was in my head and discarding it. We learn from everything we do. Maintaining momentum is very important.❖

Interview:

CARLA ADAMS

ARTIST: PERTH, AUSTRALIA

CHALLENGE & SUBVERT

How's the journey been?

I have a background in photography but I haven't touched a camera in years. It came to a point where my ideas weren't being serviced by the medium of photography so I decided to go back to art school as a "mature aged student." Now I guess I'm a painter but I do a lot of textile work too.

Your art is very tactile. But a lot of your subjects come from the impersonal online world?

I don't actually think the internet is impersonal at all. I am making work about those intimate encounters you might have with a web cam performer or someone on tinder or okcupid. I'm less interested in mass attended online spaces - I like those one-on-one encounters. I get asked about the tactility of my work a lot and it has a lot to do with the way we use these online platforms. We hold smart phones in our hands and dirty them up with finger prints and make up smears, our computers get hot in our laps There are some very tactile things about personal devices.

How did you find your point of view - Killer Idea as an artist?

Through lots and lots of research and thinking. I might have one of those "light bulb" moments in the shower or on the bus - those times where ideas just pop into your head but they often need supporting and contextualising with research. Research could be reading, trying different methods of making, looking at other artists or trying dating apps. I tend to spend a very long time on dating platforms.

PHOTO: PETER CHENG

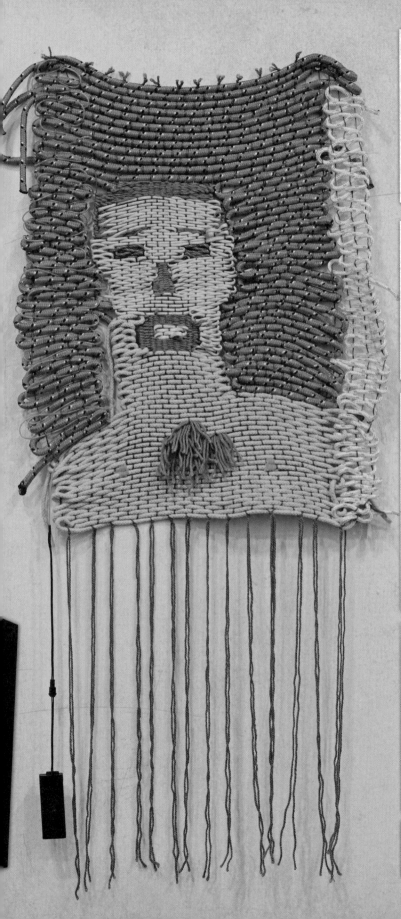

What are the major themes you're dealing with?

My work figures out ways I can challenge the male gaze and subvert gendered online behaviour. I also question things like craft, kitsch and "women's work." I like to tease out online moments and make them into something tangible and real.

What inspires you?

I get inspiration from my artist friends, seeing them succeed makes me want that for myself. Instagram is pretty good too. I think it's important to go to a lot of art shows in your city. I like to look at work and ask myself "how could this work relate to my practice?"

Describe your creative process?

I spend a lot of time on dating sites and apps, learning to be both a spectator and a player. Lots of screen snaps and notes and taken and these make their way into the studio and get turned into drawings or plans for paintings or textile work. Sometimes things don't work out or aren't what I imagined but I think that is just part of the process, you just have to keep going.

If you get stuck, how do you keep going?

I put things down and get out of the studio. Sometimes a break and "fresh" eyes are all you need to work out what needs changing. Treating studio time like a job helps me too, I wouldn't just leave work if something went wrong, I would work to solve the problem.

Best advice?

Making something is better than making nothing.❖

Interview:

NICK ONKEN

PHOTOGRAPHER: N.Y. U.S.

CREATE YOUR MOMENTS

What are you hunting?

That's a big question. It's a journey of creativity and discovery. I started as a graphic designer, so I believe that gave me the base understanding and appreciation for design which plays into every aspect of what I'm doing now. I never thought I would be a photographer when I started but I found it and fell in love with making pictures. It was a fast, not so fast journey to the here and now. The creative journey is a long one, and is constantly evolving. It took me a good 5 years of practicing photography to get to the place were people were paying me high dollars to produce advertising quality imagery. Constant practice in developing my creative eye and vision. Even to this day, I am constantly shooting new work to become better and better. Now my projects are expanding beyond photography into hand drawn type and building a brand. I've also started a podcast, Shoptalk Radio where I interview successful creative entrepreneurs on this very question.

What inspires you?

Life inspires me. Creating cool things inspires me. Great conversations inspire me. Travel inspires me. So many things, but primarily new experiences of these sorts. I'm grateful that I get to wake up every day and create what I want and dream of. It's the beauty of the choices I made when I began this journey.

PHOTOS: NICK ONKEN

Life lessons learnt?

Recently on my trip to Cuba, I photographed this granny that had so much youthful optimism, it inspired me to keep finding that and living that for myself. We only have one life. Why not have fun the whole way through?

What's your killer idea?

Recently I've been creating the mission of my mantra/hashtag #CreateYourMoments Every thing in life is a choice. You may not be able to choose where you come from or what you're dealt with, but you can certainly choose what you do with it. Life is a mental game in every aspect of it. You can learn to become better at life. My quest is to inspire everyone that we can create what we want in life by following that spark and dedicating ourselves to getting there. The biggest difference between humans is the way we think, and the gap between dreaming and doing.

Biggest obstacle on the creative journey?

My biggest obstacle in life, is my own mind. I realized over the last couple years how much of a fear of judgement I've been walking around with my whole life. It's inhibited conversations that could have been had and other opportunities from being in too much of a shell. I'm working on breaking that cycle now but it can be difficult to break patterns from our upbringing. ❖

Climb up high
into a tree.
Find a place
where you feel free.

Look down upon
the world below.
Until from the soul
emotions flow.

Then target the thing
that grabs your eye.
To capture culture
you must fly.

DIETER RAMS ➤ INDUSTRIAL DESIGN

TRAP

VINCE FROST ➤ GRAPHIC DESIGN

COCO & BREEZY ➜ FASHION DESIGN

PERS

ACHA BARBER ➜ AUTOMOTIVE DESIGN

TRAPPING THE KILLER IDEA

To trap a Killer Idea fundamentally requires a well designed trap. In this case, the term "design" refers to both the process and the product. The two are intrinsically linked; you can only capture prey if the trap is well designed, therefore functioning as it is intended. And it will only be well designed if a robust design process has been adhered to, taking into account a myriad of factors:

1. The hunter observes the quarry (target audience) and researches its peculiarities and behaviours.

2. The correct bait is selected. This is highly important as this is what will entice the quarry.

3. The trap is designed through a process of concepting, crafting and prototyping. This process is repeated and refined as often as required until the best design is found, at which point it can then be built.

4. The trap is then positioned in the environment where the quarry is likely to frequent. If the trap functions effectively, by regularly and systematically capturing the desired quarry, then the trap itself may also be considered to be the embodiment of a Killer Idea.

THE TRAPPING PROCESS

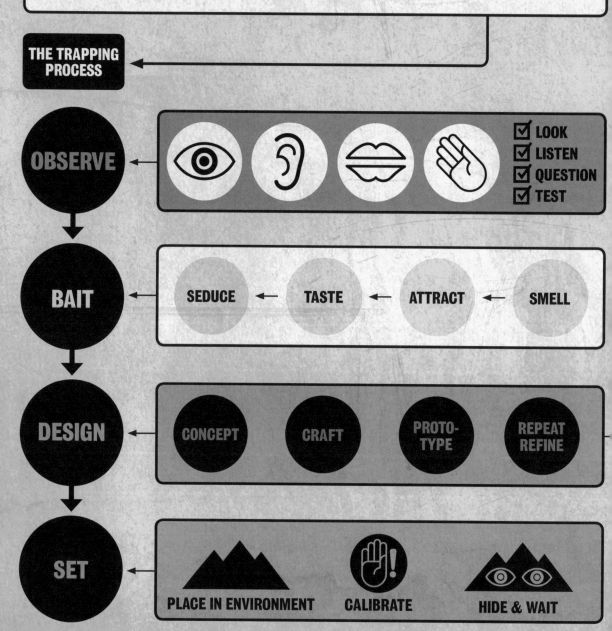

OBSERVE

☑ LOOK
☑ LISTEN
☑ QUESTION
☑ TEST

BAIT

SEDUCE ← TASTE ← ATTRACT ← SMELL

DESIGN

CONCEPT · CRAFT · PROTO-TYPE · REPEAT REFINE

SET

PLACE IN ENVIRONMENT · CALIBRATE · HIDE & WAIT

BAIT

The bait is what lures the quarry toward the trap. It is the designer's task to identify what the target audience is most likely to find appetising. The ingredients are discovered during the observation phase of the process, when attitudes, patterns of behaviour and other mating rituals are recorded. This requires looking, listening, asking questions and testing theories until a unique insight into what the quarry truly desires is discovered.

The bait will be a combination of sensory and emotional ingredients which when blended in correct proportions act like an aphrodisiac to attract the quarry. It essentially becomes the core idea or the heart and soul, around which the trap can be designed.

DESIRES

ATTITUDE

IDENTITY

LOVE

SPIRIT

VITALITY

VALUES

BELIEFS

BUILD: FUNCTION

A common misconception about design is that the quality is determined through aesthetics alone. In fact, it is functionality that is of more importance.

Once this is understood, a trap can be designed and built so that its aesthetic form is determined through its functional requirements.

TRAP

BAIT

QUARRY

BUILD: FORM

The functional requirements of the trap are that it holds the bait in place and operates effectively when triggered.

Aesthetic considerations (the form of the trap) should reinforce this. Either to lure in the prey or to effectively appear invisible so as not to distract from the bait.

The concept for this spread inspired by 'Ten Principles for Good Design'. By Dieter Rams.

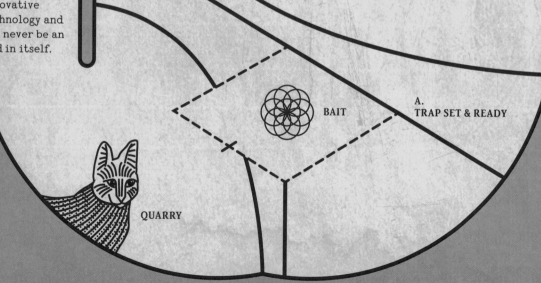

"

1
GOOD DESIGN IS INNOVATIVE

Technological development is always offering new opportunities for innovative design. But innovative design always develops in tandem with innovative technology and can never be an end in itself.

2
GOOD DESIGN MAKES A PRODUCT USEFUL

A product is bought to be used. It has to satisfy certain criteria, not only functional, but also psychological and aesthetic. Good design emphasises the usefulness of a product whilst disregarding anything that could possibly detract from it.

3
GOOD DESIGN IS AESTHETIC

The aesthetic quality of a product is integral to its usefulness because products we use every day affect our person and our wellbeing. But only well executed objects can be beautiful.

4
GOOD DESIGN IS UNOBTRUSIVE

Products fulfilling a purpose are like tools. They are neither decorative objects nor works of art. Their design should therefore be both neutral and restrained, to leave room for the user's self-expression.

5
GOOD DESIGN MAKES A PRODUCT UNDERSTANDABLE

It clarifies the product's structure. Better still, it can make the product talk. At best, it is self-explanatory.

BAIT

A.
TRAP SET & READY

QUARRY

German industrial designer Dieter Rams identified ten key principles which can be used to determine if a design is good or not. These principles are now celebrated across all design disciplines and are therefore applicable to trapping the Killer Idea.

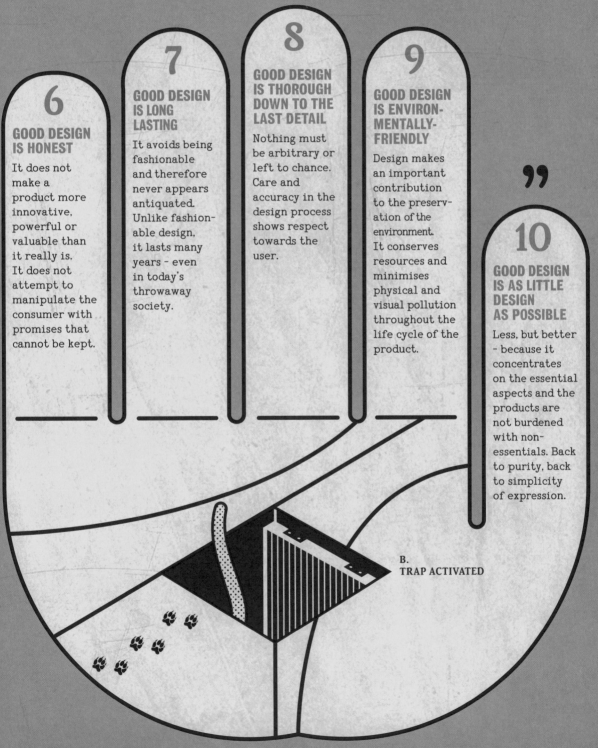

6

GOOD DESIGN IS HONEST

It does not make a product more innovative, powerful or valuable than it really is. It does not attempt to manipulate the consumer with promises that cannot be kept.

7

GOOD DESIGN IS LONG LASTING

It avoids being fashionable and therefore never appears antiquated. Unlike fashion-able design, it lasts many years – even in today's throwaway society.

8

GOOD DESIGN IS THOROUGH DOWN TO THE LAST DETAIL

Nothing must be arbitrary or left to chance. Care and accuracy in the design process shows respect towards the user.

9

GOOD DESIGN IS ENVIRON-MENTALLY-FRIENDLY

Design makes an important contribution to the preserv-ation of the environment. It conserves resources and minimises physical and visual pollution throughout the life cycle of the product.

10

GOOD DESIGN IS AS LITTLE DESIGN AS POSSIBLE

Less, but better – because it concentrates on the essential aspects and the products are not burdened with non-essentials. Back to purity, back to simplicity of expression.

B.
TRAP ACTIVATED

COCO AND BREEZY

FASHION/PRODUCT DESIGN
N.Y. U.S.

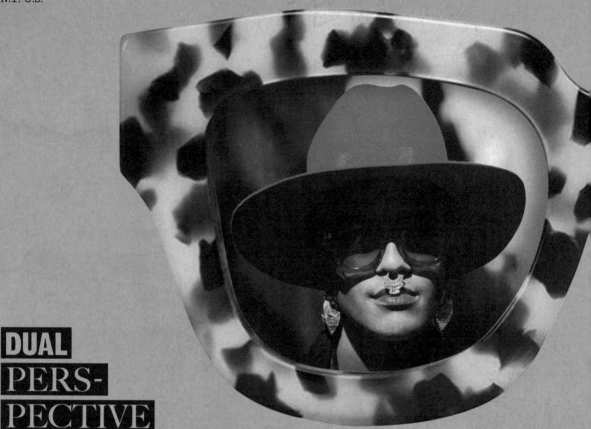

DUAL PERS- PECTIVE

Where have you come from?

We came from the suburbs in Minnesota. We were those kids that always knew we were different. We did not relate to anyone nor had the resources around us for things we wanted to do. We started working and have been financially on our own since we were 15 years old. With things like that being a part of our life, it made us the hard working women that we are today. Since we did not grow up with a lot of resources we had to create our own resources. We moved to NYC with nothing but a dream, passion, no money saved but the crazy mindset that we could change the world. With any hardships or challenges, we always had the mindset to find the positive in it. We use every situation to help us grow. We feel like it takes a certain mindset to be an entrepreneur and we are the essence of that.

What's been the biggest challenge?

The biggest challenge in our journey has been balancing our personal and work life. We love our work so much that it doesn't feel like work. But we are very aware that it is healthy to find balance. We have been pushing ourselves to be even more productive with our time management so that we can get a little personal time to free our mind for even more room for ideas.

Do you have a philosophy which guides your work?

We are always finding new ways of self improvement and practising positive energy. We live by this quote "Don't stress about situations you can't change … find the solution." When you are an entrepreneur you go through a lot of challenges, so you really have to train your mind how to handle them without letting them break you down.

What does the Coco and Breezy brand stand for?

The Coco and Breezy brand is not only eyewear, but we have built a lifestyle around the brand. We create original designs that are fun and cool, but most importantly functional with great quality. We are representative of the generation of millennials in design and entrepreneurship. We believe in creating our own rules and collaboration to show new waves in the market.

What inspires your work?

We are artists. That is a big inspiration in our work. Being artists, we have a lot of mediums. We love to paint, draw, dance and DJ music. All of these elements give us a lot of inspiration in the creation of our collections. We also travel a lot, so a lot of our eyewear designs are inspired by architecture we see while travelling.

Describe your creative process?

Our creative process includes pulling inspiration from all of our creative outlets and mashing them together. We love jamming, DJ'ing and rocking out to music - as we feel like that is when our creative juices start pumping. I always carry a sketch book everywhere I go, as I feel like the world is my inspiration.

We love to paint and that is where our colour inspiration comes from. When designing our eyewear, it starts off with Breezy hand-sketching my ideas out while jamming to music. Next, we illustrate the sketch into a digital form. Now, this is where it gets technical ... we have to create specs and call out all of the measurements for each piece of the eyewear. When that is confirmed our business partner Duane adds the drawing into autocad and Coco and Duane make the final decisions on the designs.

How do you break mental blocks?

Being an entrepreneur your journey is like a roller coaster. You have your ups and downs. I think those down times are really important because it gives us time to reflect and make

pivots. We analyse certain things in our life to see what's adding to our productivity and throw away things that are taking away from it. During mental blocks, we like to put ourselves in new environments and change our daily routines. This helps open new parts of the mind.

What's the best piece of advice you've ever received?

To always be ourselves. When we first started our business at 19, we were going into big corporate offices for meetings and we didn't know if we should change our personal style. Then this one man told us, "always stay true to yourself, that's why people are taking meetings with you." Now we go into meetings staying true to our look while holding intellectual conversations. ✤

Interview:

SACHA BARBER

AUTOMOTIVE DESIGN.
TURIN, ITALY.

KIND
AFFLICTION

What is it that made you always want to design for Alfa Romeo?

When I was three years old my dad bought his first of many Alfas; a 116 Giulietta. Since then I was hooked on cars and Alfa Romeos in particular.

I always loved drawing when I was young and drew cars for as long as I can remember. So it was my dream from an early age to design cars for Alfa Romeo.

Is there a vision or philosophy which guides the aesthetic?

There is a great quote by Orazio Satta, one of Alfa Romeos most celebrated engineers from the 1960s and 1970s in which he talked about Alfa Romeo being more than just a mere car factory, but rather a way of life, or even a

kind of affliction. He related to it as total enthusiasm for this form of transport, a company more related to the irrational human heart rather than the brain. I thinks it's interesting to hear those sort of sentiments coming from an engineer.

A beautiful Alfa Romeo is composed of pure volumes, sensual sections, clean surfaces. It shouldn't resort to fussy details or random graphic signs on the body. The design should also reflect the car's dynamic qualities: it's lightness, agility and performance.

What inspires your work?

We have an incredible heritage to draw inspiration from. This can be a help but also at times be a

burden as we have to respect that heritage. Some of my favourite Alfas that I will often look to for inspiration are the Zagato TZ models, Bertone's Giulia Coupè (by Giugiaro), Scaglione's 33 Stradale, and even more recent mass produced models such as the 156 from 1997 which managed beautifully to distil Alfa Romeo's DNA into a modern 4-door saloon.

I also like to drive just for the sake of driving when I get the chance. The designers in Alfa often go to drive in the Alps near Turin with our interesting cars (there are all sorts). My old, modified, noisy Alfa GTV is a good companion in the mountains and driving fast on a beautiful empty mountain road can clear my head, reignite my passion and remind me why I love these cars.

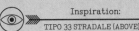
Inspiration:
TIPO 33 STRADALE (ABOVE)
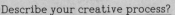

Describe your creative process?

We sketch for ideation. We sketch on paper with biros, pencils and markers. In the past renderings were hand coloured but now we scan our sketches and render them on the computer or else sketch/render directly onto our WACOM Cintiqs. Once the direction of the design has been decided we proceed with a 3D CAS model or a physical scale model.

If you get stuck, what do you do?

I try not to panic. I usually look at some older work of mine that I like, to reassure myself of what I'm capable of when things are going well. And I find that some physical exercise helps to clear the mind and stay positive, I usually cycle the 10km to work.

What does "design" mean to you?

Design for me is my work every day: researching, analysing, sketching, rendering, putting tapes on a model, observing, sculpting, collaborating with modellers, engineers, project managers, presenting drawings and models. The work is very varied depending on the stage of the project you're working on. After that long process hopefully you've got a nice, satisfying result to show for it. Regarding the balance between form and function, that's a compromise we have to constantly contend with. The designer will often want the roof as low as possible, the wheels big and pumped out, the side glass to be as slim and sleek as possible. But as the design progresses we have

to take in to account all sorts of feasibility factors such as ingress/egress, driver and passenger accommodation and visibility, the visibility angles and layout for the headlights and tail lights, Even the position of a simple door hinge underneath the body can have a big impact on the style and sculpture you can achieve on the body side. So the real skill of a car designer, apart from doing the initial sketch which is selected, is just as much being able to navigate all these constraints while keeping the original intention of the sketch alive.

Best advice you ever received?

"Just do your best and don't worry" - Morrissey ♣

NATURE
PROVIDES

The natural world provides a brilliant source of inspiration. If you look closely, you'll find all sorts of clues for making effective design.

The size, shape and silhouette of animals have long provided inspiration for the curves, lines and other dynamic qualities found in industrial product design.

In another example, Apple's Jony Ives observed how a raindrop retains its form when resting on a surface. This became the inspiration for the iconic and ground breaking design of the Macintosh mouse, which embodied the curved aesthetic of a single drop of rainwater.

Now, let us consider some of the design qualities of the infamous Venus flytrap.

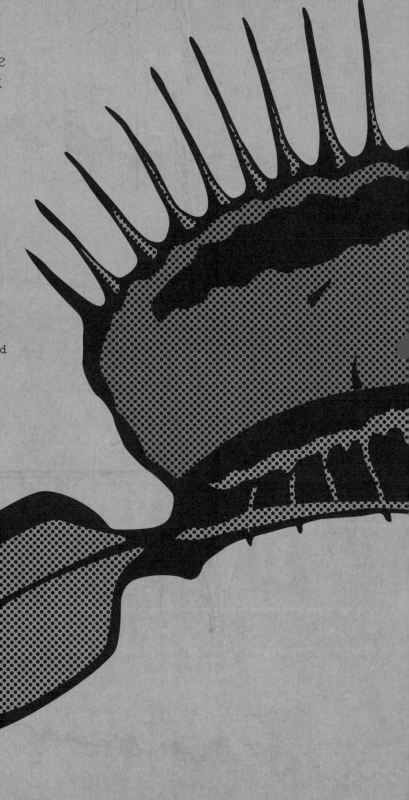

BRAND IDENTITY:

Brand name:
Venus flytrap (Dionaea muscipula)
Named after the Roman goddess
of love.

Brand positioning:
Carnivorous plant native to
subtropical wetlands on the East
Coast of the United States.

Brand promise:
'Come on in baby, I'll show you a
good time.'

Target audience:
Insects and spiders.

Bait:
The leaves forming the trap
secrete a sweet nectar that draws
in insects searching for food.

Design:
The trapping mechanism is
tripped when prey contacts one
of the three hair-like trichomes
that are found on the upper
surface of each of the lobe,
causing the lobes to snap shut.
The edges are fringed with 'cilia',
which mesh together and prevent
large prey from escaping.

Thus, the functionality of the
design has determined the
Venus flytrap's unique and
distinctive form.

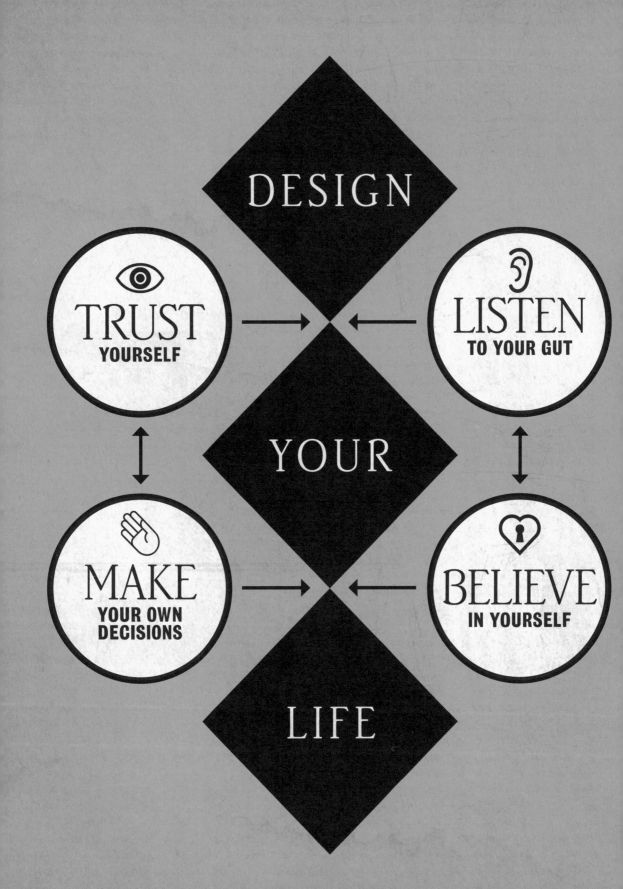

DESIGN

TRUST
YOURSELF

LISTEN
TO YOUR GUT

YOUR

MAKE
YOUR OWN
DECISIONS

BELIEVE
IN YOURSELF

LIFE

The strategic thought which underpins the design process is usually applied to solving business problems. In his book, *Design Your Life*, graphic designer Vince Frost demonstrates how the underlying principles of great design and fresh creativity can be applied not only to a brand or product — but to life itself.

You say 'Trust yourself. Listen to your gut. Make your own decisions. Believe in yourself'.

I was going through a bit of a crisis just as I was about to put the book to print and I talked to my mentor. I was having all these self doubts and she sent me a message which was so appropriate, and in a way it was a good summary of all the things I needed to do; a summary of the book and I guess it is that we might sort of think differently, to believe in yourself, to trust yourself. It's fine to have doubts and people will often have those but it sends a simple clear message or messages that are I guess in a way. In our busy hectic lives we kind of get sidetracked and get distracted from understanding ourselves and for me this kind of reminded me to stop, focus, trust and believe in the inner voice. Believe in what you believe in and get on with it.

Tell me about the process of extracting ideas from design and applying them to living life.

Well I guess that it kind of came as a revelation for me or a realisation, that for years and years, for probably just getting on for 30 years now, the designing and redesigning everything about myself and putting 99% of my energy into my work and into my career, which I love, and I tried all kinds of things. I would always wait until I was in a bad situation; like you know, stress beyond belief, or exhaustion, or was sick and then I would go to somebody else and ask them for advice on how to fix myself and they would then prescribe something, say "do this" or "do that" It wasn't until I kind of had that revelation of going "you know, actually my life is the biggest and most important design project I will ever have" and I have never really seen my life in that way. I just sort of saw it as being... a lot of the stuff was just an inconvenience or my body was meant to function no matter what it did. But the reality is that I needed to take myself seriously as I do with a design brief - understand what the brief or the problem is and work on a plan for coming up with a solution for that. I guess that would be pretty straight forward for some people but for me it was like, wow, shit that's actually "why didn't I ever think like that before" and since I have done that I have tackled my life as if it was a design project, every time and it is not easy but I think differently about my life and then act differently about how I resolve things.

Life is much like the creative process; there are highs and lows. How does that inform your creativity?

Well everything that we do, whether it is paid for or not, my belief and my desire is that we are helping people to be better. Organisations, large and small charities, individuals, whatever it is, we are designing a successful outcome for them and so that is my objective. That's the reason for being in business and I am determined with my team to ensure that we create that outcome. So we are not out doing stuff, doing design. In a way we are much more strategic in how we are thinking about how we create the most successful outcome with every single job that we do. The outcome is firstly our client's success; so what is it that is going to make a difference to them? How are they going to communicate to their desired target audience? How do we work out who their desired target audience is? How do we pinpoint that to ensure that we create the best stimulus and the best ideas to trigger a reaction, whether it is to buy something, engage in an environment or to communicate with the audience. That's what we aim to do. You have an alternative with every single project you have, you have an opportunity to make the world a better place and that may sound very earnest saying that but I just believe there is so much man made crap in this world, that nature and the world itself is so incredibly beautiful and special. I feel I have an obligation that anything we put into this world which is man made needs to be basically more sustainable or adding value to people's lives - not just junk. ⟩⟩→

" FINDING A

SOLUTION

FROM WITHIN THE

PROBLEM

THAT'S A BIG DIFFERENCE **"**

You say "question everything", tell me a bit about that?

That's kind of the key thing, questioning everything is very important for me and that is about listening, about digging deep. It is about really immersing yourself in the potential problem so don't come at it from a superficial level. Don't just kind of go with the first thing you think about, you have got to really engage in the opportunity and learn much more about it. I find that the more I know about a problem... actually the best thing is if I walk into an opportunity and I know nothing about it, I used to be quite embarrassed or awkward about that and feel like I should know something. But I actually see that as a huge benefit if I don't know anything about it; it doesn't mean I'm stupid, it just means that I'm now on a quick learning curve, I've got fresh eyes on this thing and I can learn quite quickly about all the ins and outs of this opportunity I can come back with insights that other clients can't see as they are so much immersed in the day to day of it so that is something which I find is critical to finding the clues for the project or find the clues which will help you with the solutions that will come from that project. Again, also by doing that I am not just imposing solutions on to a problem. I'm actually finding a solution from within the problem. And that is a big difference.

You say, "explore the unknown" but interestingly you also note that the comfort zone is your place to recharge before stepping outside of it.

The key thing I have learned is don't try to be perfect, don't try to fix everything at once but to work on incremental steps towards it so it is more like the age old approach of, you know, start to do things, sort of put things down, start to make processes through trial and error and just by "doing". That can make a huge difference to me because otherwise I just leave it in my head and it becomes this huge kind of growing thing and gets out of control. So I need to start seeing it coming into the world and start seeing it kind of living. I guess in the past to try and make it perfect I would think I will keep it in my head until it is absolutely worked out and then I will put it down and try it etc. I think what I have learned is

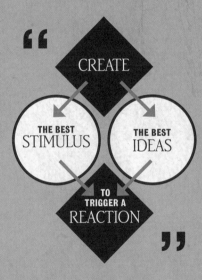

to stop procrastinating and get on with it. Maybe go for a walk, maybe get some other kind of stimulus, maybe try different ways of approaching things to create a fresh solution.

What's your Killer Idea?

Basically it kind of came from me hitting the wall too many times. I'm fifty, which I don't feel is very old, but I realised that "hang on a minute, I am well over half way now". I started off as a young designer and I had the whole world. I had no idea of time – you don't know when you are going to be finished. It all seemed endless. When I was about 45 I had nervous breakdowns or mid life crises, but it was just in terms of my thinking "I need to do things better". The way that I was working and living, drinking and eating too much of the wrong thing, not exercising enough or ad hoc, working 20 hour days. All this kind of stuff seemed like a lifetime career of working at that kind of pace and it just wasn't sustainable and no wonder every so often I would just hit a wall and crumble and think I'm going to die at the extreme, I just thought I need to fix this. I cannot continue like this any longer. It is not good for me.

So really my Killer Idea was about sustaining my life. Sustaining my wellbeing and realising that I love what I do, I love my life, I love my kids and my partner and everything. I have got so many great things I am grateful for and I needed to focus on myself. I thought I was focusing on my wellbeing but I was just focusing on giving so much out because I wanted to help every situation. Everything was a problem that needed to be fixed and it became too overwhelming when I wasn't in a good place myself physically.

So that is when I started to think, "okay I need to do what people say; eat vegetables every day, need to exercise, need to sleep well." All these things I thought yeah, I will park that, I will do that when I've got time or when I am retired. It's just not sustainable and I wish in a way – maybe this is how life is – I wish that I had established that much earlier on because I think I would've had a more balanced life and had a lot more healthier lifestyle.

I don't regret anything but I just think that life is all about learning. Learning new ways of doing things better.❖

There's nothing that
you can't conceive.
If you know what
you want to achieve.

Sketch and concept
'til it's designed.
Construct with care
once it's refined.

Then set the trap
and lie in wait.
For the killer idea
to take the bait.

HUNTERS

GEORGE LOIS

DAVID THOMASON

AD VERTERE {LATIN} "TO TURN TOWARDS"

Out of all the professions where creativity is a prerequisite, there is no other industry that demands such a constant flow of ideas as advertising.

The men and women who work in it are tasked with using creativity to sell products and brands in a highly competitive environment, in such a way that their ideas will get cut-through, shape conversation, stir emotions and change behaviour.

In other words, they're Head Hunters. They attract eye balls, seduce ears, capture attention and imagination.

They do this by penetrating the head and hitting the heart.

Every scalp taken represents an item purchased, brand loved or viral idea shared. In a society driven by consumerism this is big business and the competition to take a scalp is immense.

In this chapter Ad-legend Dave Trott gives us the run down on Predatory Thinking. Ad-Gods George Lois, Paul Arden and David Ogilvy's insights on ideas are worshipped. And a Head Hunter from down under, David Thomason, explains how the head and heart are important but it is behaviour that's the real target.❖

"We know that £18.3bn is spent on all forms of advertising and marketing every year. We know tha 4% is remembered positively, 7% i remembered negatively, and 89% isn noticed or remembere

Dave Tro

2

COMMUNICATION
THE GENERAL THRUST, PROVIDING
THE IMPORTANT INFORMATION.

4A. GETS NOTICED
4B. REMEMBERED
4C. LIKED **IMPACT** **4**

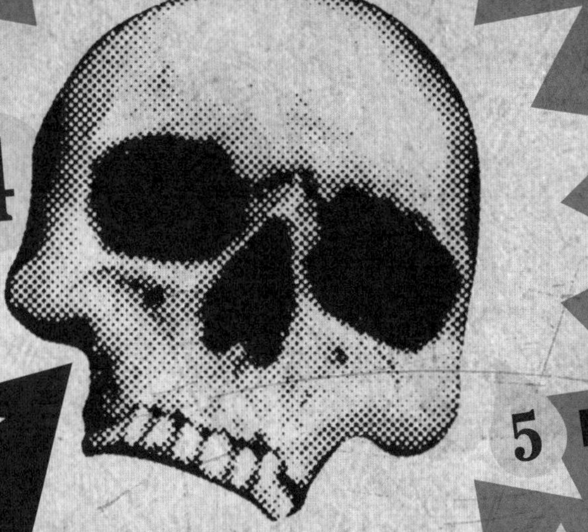

3

CREATIVE

EXECUTION
{IDEA LACED IN VENOM}

IDEA
{THE SHARP END}

INSIGHT

THE LEADING FORCE IS PROVIDED THROUGH POWERFUL INSIGHT INTO HUMAN NATURE

5 EFFECT

AWARENESS

KNOWLEDGE

LIKING

PREFERENCE

CONVICTION

ACTUAL PURCHASE

The Hierarchy of Effects, Clow and Baack.

{SCALPED!}

And that, my friend, is how you take a scalp in advertising.

STRATEGY

1

THE HUNTER MUST PLAN TO BE IN THE RIGHT PLACE, AT THE RIGHT TIME, TARGETING THE RIGHT HEADS, WITH THE RIGHT MESSAGE, TO SOLVE THE RIGHT PROBLEM.

DAVE TROTT

PREDATORY
THINKING

No matter what problem you may face, keep one thing in mind at all time: Nothing exists in limbo. That is to say, every problem, barrier or obstacle to you getting what you want is connected to something else. Is connected to many other things - physical, social, financial, personal. It don't matter. Once you've grasped this fact, you can go about solving the problem.

But not by rearranging the thing right in front of your face. No dear. By going upstream. By looking at the bigger picture. By looking at the context.

Once you've worked out what the context is, then you can go about changing the context - to change the problem you really want fixed. But you gotta get up there and find which piece of the puzzle is the weak link. The most important. Or the singular element which defines everything else.

You say "get upstream to
change the context". For most
of us the problem is that at
any given time we're in a lake
with multiple streams feeding
into it. Up to our eyeballs in
financial issues, personal or
creative challenges. Any tips
for deciphering which stream
to follow?

Bill Bernbach said "Principals
endure, formulas don't"

Any formula for being creative
can't be creative by definition.

If there was a formula we
could feed it into a computer.

The creativity is in choosing
where and how to get
upstream.

The creativity is in the
unexpected. ⟫→

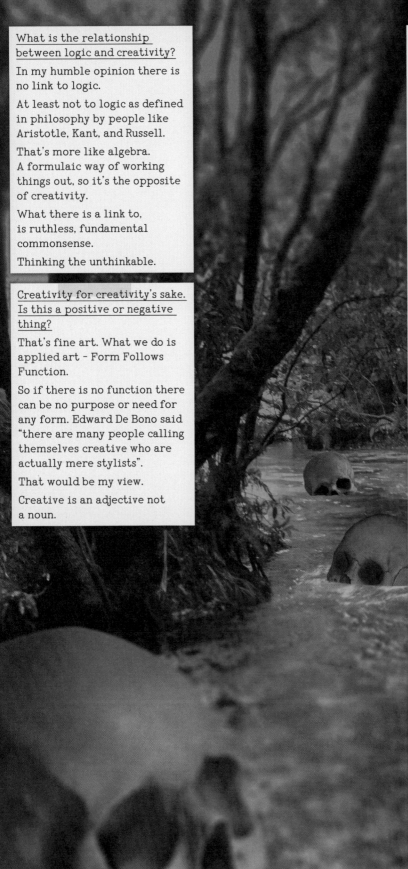

What is the relationship between logic and creativity?

In my humble opinion there is no link to logic.

At least not to logic as defined in philosophy by people like Aristotle, Kant, and Russell.

That's more like algebra. A formulaic way of working things out, so it's the opposite of creativity.

What there is a link to, is ruthless, fundamental commonsense.

Thinking the unthinkable.

Creativity for creativity's sake. Is this a positive or negative thing?

That's fine art. What we do is applied art – Form Follows Function.

So if there is no function there can be no purpose or need for any form. Edward De Bono said "there are many people calling themselves creative who are actually mere stylists".

That would be my view.

Creative is an adjective not a noun.

When you're hunting the killer idea and the track goes cold, what do you do?

People say "stop trying to reinvent the wheel".

But that's exactly what we have to do, reinvent the wheel every time.

That's difficult and uncomfortable, like a miner looking for a fresh seam.

You try everything until something works.

I read books, read magazines, watch documentaries, go to art galleries, have conversations, get drunk.

If everything fails I give up.

I try to get someone else to do the job, or I do a responsible (but uncreative) job this time.

And hope the next brief is better.

Some times you can't win pretty, you have to win ugly.

Every person is capable of hunting their own personal Killer Idea. Is Predatory Thinking yours?

Predatory Thinking is just the name for the way I've always worked.

Murray Chick (our planning partner) gave it that name because he said it made it more saleable for the agency.

It's just street smarts elevated to marketing, or whatever you're doing.

I learned it growing up in east London, I learned it even more later on in New York.

It's just how to out think people.

If we want something, we must take it from someone else.

Most people (especially English, middle class people) refuse to believe that.

Which is why they aren't very good at what they do. ❖

Dave Trott's blog has gained a cult following due to insightful musings, such as this one:

MAKE FEAR YOUR FRIEND

"In 2006 Apple's revenues were $19 billion.

The iPod alone was $7.7 billion of that, it had 90% of the personal music-player market.

Things were looking good. So why did Steve Jobs wake up in a sweat?

Why did he start writing numbers down, making phone calls, rushing into work the next day arranging meetings and cancelling projects?

Why did Steve Jobs think he had to avert a crisis?

Well precisely because things were looking good. The previous day, Steve Jobs had seen the new Nokia mobile phone.

No big deal, just another mobile phone: It had the usual range of trivial features.

One of the gimmicks was you could download six tunes onto it. Not very useful, no one cared.

But something at the back of Steve's mind nagged away at him.

And he woke up in the middle of the night thinking "If they can download six tunes what happens if they can download sixty tunes? Or six hundred tunes? That's the end of the iPod - that's fifty percent of our business gone - It'll be too late to worry then, we won't have a company."

And he started writing down numbers, doing calculations, and as far as he could see there was only one answer.

So he started making phone calls, organising meetings and cancelling projects.

The next morning he got his people together and he said "We're getting into the phone business".

Naturally they thought he was crazy, he was being paranoid. But he explained they had no choice.

Either they ate Nokia's lunch, or Nokia would eat theirs.

So in 2007 Apple launched the iPhone.

By 2009 the iPod still made up $8 billion of their revenue, but the iPhone was nearly $7 billion.

By 2013 the iPod had dropped to $2.3 billion of revenue, but the iPhone had grown to $91 billion.

Apple is now the world's largest smart phone manufacturer.

Nokia, who Steve Jobs was scared stiff of, barely exists anymore.

Mainly because he was frightened and they weren't.

He knew that fear is the most valuable tool an entrepreneur can have.

Fear will give you an edge on the competition.

Recently I was reading that fear is one of the great strengths of species that evolve.

Suppose you can't tell the shape of a bear from a rock.

If you always assume the shape is a rock most times you will be right, and you'll lead a more relaxed life.

Right until the time you're wrong and it actually is a bear.

Then you die a painful death.

But suppose you always assume that shape is a bear, and you run.

Most times you will be wrong, because it actually is a rock.

But the one time it really is a bear, you'll survive.

So species that respect and cultivate fear are the ones that survive.

They learn to make fear their unfair advantage.

They are more aware, more attentive, and have an edge over the competition.

Like Steve Jobs, they know fear is their friend."

davetrott.campaignlive.co.uk • March 11, 2015

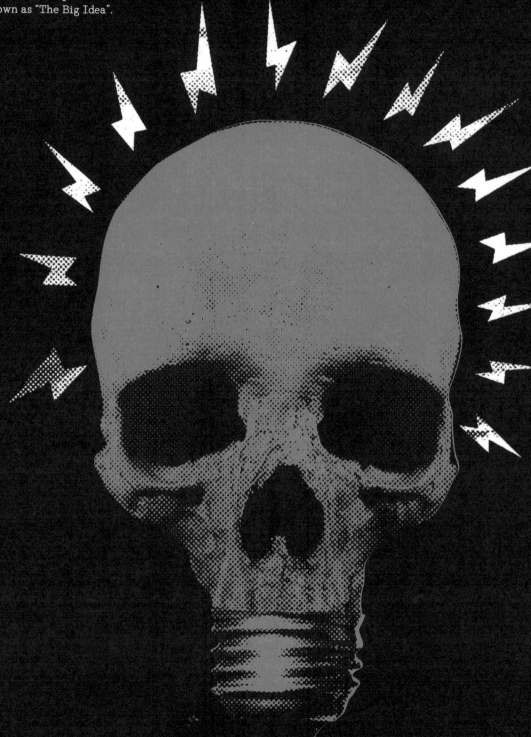

All quotes on this spread are from 'Damn Good Advice' by George Lois.

THE BIG IDEA

"The Big Idea in advertising sears the virtues of a product into a viewer's brain and heart, resulting in a sales explosion. To be a master communicator, words and images must catch people's eyes, penetrate the minds, warm their hearts and cause them to act!"

BETTER TO BE RECKLESS THAN CAREFUL. BETTER TO BE BOLD THAN SAFE."

"I never create ideas. I discover them - snared from the air as they float by me. So if you're trying to achieve greatness, go out into the world and sail the ocean blue and live a life of discovery."

"A trend is always a trap. The fact that others are moving in a certain direction is always proof positive, that a new direction is the only direction."

"THE POINT ABOUT UNUSUAL IDEAS HAS TO BE THEIR

PROXIMITY TO MADNESS

If you have what you consider a fantastic concept, you must drive it to the precipice.

If you don't take it to the edge, you've chickened out.

PUSH YOUR THOUGHT TO THE VERY RIM OF

INSANITY"

"Great graphic and verbal communication depends on understanding and adapting to the culture, anticipating the culture, criticizing changes in the culture, and helping to change the culture. Any entrepreneur, inventor, artist... who instinctively feels the way to go is against a conservative, indoctrinated society and bucks the trend, and who understands the zeitgeist of the time - your mission is not to sedate, but to awaken, to disturb, to communicate, to command, to instigate, and even to provoke."

"SAFE CONVENTIONAL WORK IS A TICKET TO OBLIVION.

Great creativity should stun, by presenting the viewer with an idea that seemingly suspends conventions of understanding.

IN THAT SWIFT INTERVAL BETWEEN

SHOCK & REALISATION

YOU CAPTURE YOUR AUDIENCE."

PAUL ARDEN

Former creative director at Saatchi and Saatchi and author of several books. (1940 - 2008)

THERE IS NO RIGHT POINT OF VIEW

128

CONVENTIONAL

or popular point of view. There is a

LARGE

point of view which the majority share. There is a

PERSONAL

point of view.

But there is no right point of view.

You are always right. You are always wrong. It just depends from which pole you are looked at. Advances in any field are built upon by people with the small or personal point of view.

FEEL TRAPPED, STUCK, LOST?

It's not because you are making the wrong decisions, it's because you are making the right ones.

We try to make sensible decisions based on the facts in front of us.

The problem with making sensible decisions is that so is everyone else.

ou can achieve the

UNACHIEVABLE

Firstly you need to **AIM**

BEYOND

what you are capable of.

You must develop a complete disregard for where your abilities end."

8 HABITS

HABITS
OF HIGHLY CREATIVE COMMUNITIES:

Advertising agency, Ogilvy & Mather published a book called, 'The Eternal Pursuit of Unhappiness', based on founder David Ogilvy's philosophy, on how to create and preserve creative communities.

It focuses on eight behaviours, which if employed regularly, can become habitual. These habits have the power to overturn, what the ancient Greeks referred to as, a vice:

Fear, expedience, the status quo, boring, cold arithmetic, tyranny of politeness, bureaucracy and giving in.

FEAR
EXPEDIENCE
STATUS QUO
BORING
COLD ARITHMETIC
TYRANNY OF POLITENESS
BUREAUCRACY
GIVING IN

DAVID OGILVY

Founded Ogilvy & Mather and widely hailed as "the Father of Advertising". (1911-1999)

COURAGE

Ogilvy believed that fear was the most significant vice that must be overcome. He referred to it as "the demon that devours the soul." Therefore, it is courage which must be summoned, as "fear leads to self-doubt which is the chief enemy of creativity." Ogilvy saw courage as the bedrock upon which all other habits must be built. On its foundation "we begin to build the most precious commodity in the world. Trust. Then the virtuous circle begins: courage leads to trust leads to courage…"

CURIOSITY

"It is only in the open state of curiosity that we can explore, dream and make babies in our heads." Much like the "pesky 6-year-old", we have to have the courage to "ask stupid questions". If we don't, we run the risk of becoming old and stale.

PLAYFULNESS

"If necessity is the mother of invention, it is horseplay which is most certainly the father. Make it fun to work at your agency". Ogilvy knew that laughter is always the best medicine, when it comes to keeping spirits up. Because happy workers are productive workers.

CANDOUR

Being open and honest is crucial to creative problem solving. Working in an environment where frank discussions are encouraged is essential to building a creative community. To hold back your opinion is the easy option, to speak your mind is more difficult. "We only get a spark when the stone and flint are moving in opposite directions."

INTUITION

The ability to understand something intuitively, relies, not on conscious rational thought, but draws from the limitless potential of the unconscious realm. By listening to our "dreams, premonitions and gut feelings' we may get a better understanding of where it's trying to guide us. All our finest thoughts, and best ideas, are not the work of the logical mind, but gifts from the unconscious." Ogilvy believed that in a "world dominated by quarterly reports and numbers". Too much emphasis is placed on cold arithmetic at the expense of the sublime hunch.

As a result, creativity is often placed in a box and only allowed out when logic can't make any progress. The problem with this approach is that imagination provides the most creative results when it is given the free reign that only intuition allows.

FREE-SPIRITEDNESS

"Step inside a free-spirited, idea-centric company and you'll notice the air itself is different. It's called atmosphere. It's permission to practice magic: it's licence to be the best at what you are best at. The temper of the place is omnipotent and mood is everything".

Ogilvy & Mather have offices around the world and have created some of the most creative and memorable advertising of all time.

Ogilvy said "Inside a company with atmosphere, the people are not servants of the system. They are alchemists."

Could understanding that environment plays a critical role in fostering creativity be part of the secret of their success? After all, "the business of producing ideas is both tedious and terrifying."

PERSISTENCE

Ogilvy highly valued persistence as a necessary habit, required for creativity to prevail against the numerous obstacles and challenges that present themselves during the problem solving process.

Saying "zig zags, U-turns, roundabouts and loop-the-loops are all part of the creative process. You see those who live by their wits, go to work on roller coasters. The ride is exhilarating, to be sure, but one has to have a stomach of titanium."

He believed that "ignorance believe it or not is an asset. Experience and knowledge make us sensible, predictable and dull."

For Ogilvy, persistence meant that you "look, look, look" at absolutely everything as "discovery consists of seeing what every-one has seen and thinking what nobody has thought."

IDEALISM

By definition, idealism means the unrealistic pursuit of perfection. But remember, "the people who are crazy enough to think they can change the world are the ones who do." Ogilvy believed, "How great we become depends on the size of our dreams". ♣

BEHAVIOUR CHANGE

Tucked down at the bottom of the globe is an Ad agency who cottoned on early and shifted their focus from changing attitudes to changing behaviour. FCB New Zealand's Chief Strategist David Thomason developed the 'behaviour change' platform by using behavioural economics and applying principles of persuasion on a mass scale. This led to more 'emotional thinking' and has seen this remarkable little office rise from nowhere to being ranked the No.1 most effective agency in the world for *Retail* and *Government & Not For Profit* work in 2015*.

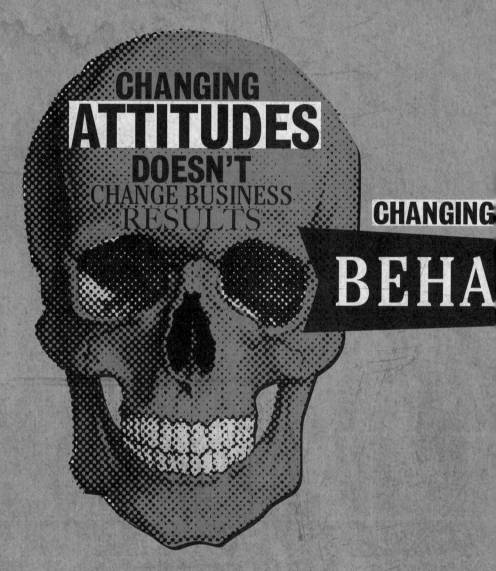

CHANGING
ATTITUDES
DOESN'T
CHANGE BUSINESS
RESULTS

CHANGING
BEHA

DAVID THOMASON

CHIEF STRATEGIST,
FCB NEW ZEALAND

AUTHORITY
We have a natural tendency to obey those placed in positions of power.

IDENTITY
We embrace a variety of identites in our lives. We signal our membership of each group through the choices we make.

HERDING
We instinctively follow the crowd, making our decisions based on what those around us are doing.

INCENTIVE
All human behaviour is driven by some sort of incentive. These incentives are not always obvious or tangible.

TO UNLOCK THE DESIRED BEHAVIOUR, 'THE ART OF **PERSUASION**' IS APPLIED.

OUR

DOES

RELATIVITY
Comparison with alternatives provides decision making shortcuts. The selection and presentation of these can influence our decisions.

LIKING
We are more likely to say yes to someone we like, admire or identify with.

SCARCITY
We assign a higher value to things that we believe are scarce. Conversely, when we perceive it to be plentiful its value falls.

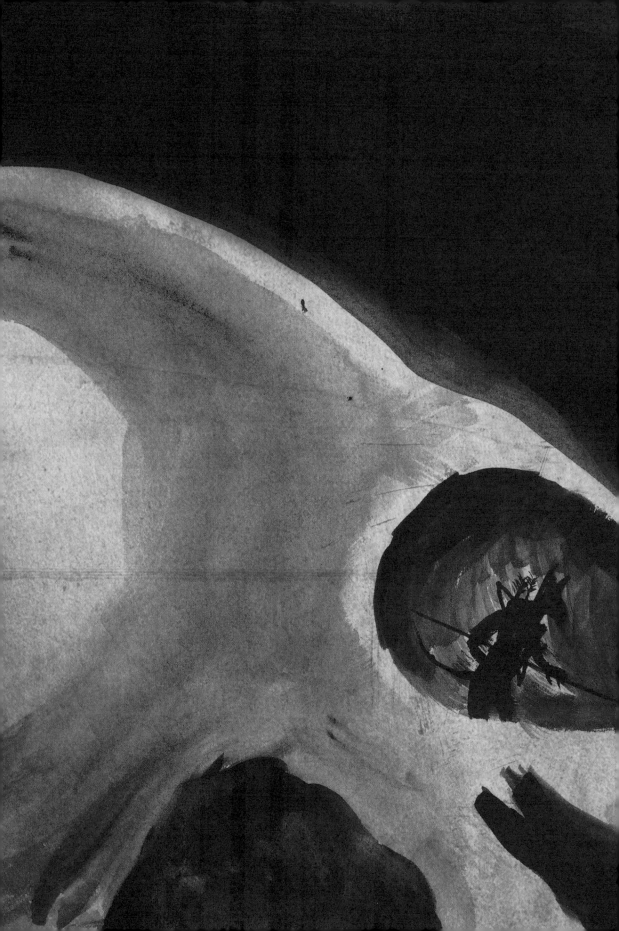

To capture eyes,
ears and mind.
And leaving not
the heart behind.

Feel the pulse
of the public.
Touch the livewire
that's electric.

Once you get
inside the skull.
The idea you wield
best not be dull.

ALBERT   E GENIUS

JE   .ITY

Surviving the Mental Environment

WE ARE BORN INTO A WORLD THAT IS ALREADY CONSUMED IN A RAGING STORM OF IDEAS. DIFFERENT RELIGIONS, CUSTOMS, CULTURES AND SOCIAL HIERARCHIES LASH ONE ANOTHER, ENSURING THAT THE BALANCE OF NATURE IS ALWAYS IN A STATE OF CONSTANT FLUX.

CLIMATE

The climate is created out of the numerous ideologies which compete, compliment and electrify one another.

Ideologies are the combination of ideals, beliefs and basic human motivations, providing a 'normative' vision of the world.

Dominant ideologies create the climate we live in, as they have power over our cognition and perception of reality.

There are two sides to the climate. That which benefits the majority of the people and the darker side which benefits only the ruling class.

Ruling class interests - "The 3Ps" are then protected by justifying ideologies such as neo liberalism.

ATMOSPHERIC PRESSURE

For the ruling elite to preserve their position at the apex of our global social hierarchy, a system of control over the dominant ideologies must be maintained.

This is engineered through control over the 3Ps. The unholy trinity of Power, Profit and Politics is the mechanism through which the Alpha ideology of "control" is exercised.

<u>Power:</u> Physical power comes in the form of military force. Soft power is achieved through control of the media and the use of propaganda. Whilst corporate power generates profit.

<u>Profits:</u> The accumulation of profit creates power and buys political influence.

Politics: Provides the authority through which decisions such as declaring war or enforcing austerity can be made.

By controlling the 3Ps, the ruling class is able to use this revolving door to maintain the dominant ideologies that create self-serving social systems.

WEATHER

Ideologies precipitate in the form of class, legal, political and economic systems which then rain down on those at ground level. Depending on your luck, in the lottery of life, you will soon discover your place in the social order. How high up you are determines if you will enjoy the warmth of wealth or the bitter cold of poverty.

SURFACE CONDITIONS

The surface conditions on the ground are largely determined by the weather above. It is here that we are raised, grow up and must discover who we are and what we have the potential to be.

To have a happy and fulfilling life, there are basic needs that must be met. If we're fortunate, we'll be surrounded by a loving and nurturing community who will help us achieve our needs.

But an individual must find their own way in life. The ability to go out into the wild and confront the problems of the world develops only once a person has reached a level of maturity, or as psychologist Abraham Maslow referred to it, 'self-actualization'.

The young hunter comes of age when both feet are planted firmly on the ground, providing the good balance required to shoot straight.

Creativity and problem solving abilities are also essential for survival beyond the safety and security of the village.

Now, suppose you were to fire an arrow and aim for the sky. How would it fly against the dominant ideologies that swirl above? Would it be sucked into the storm of consumerism and become a commodity? Would it be beaten down by the class and economic systems that prevail?

Or will you aim higher and shoot further? Do you have a Killer Idea that could pierce the dark clouds above, allowing light to shine

through on the world below?

There are still Killer Ideas whose time is yet to come, that will upend all received wisdom, common sense and convention. They will change the way we see the world - they just haven't been caught yet.

In this chapter we learn lessons from those who have braved the elements and survived under the harsher conditions of the mental environment.

Life is finite. But once you're six feet under what will live on are your ideas.

So think carefully about what it is you want to hunt in life. The world is a puzzle that wants solving. Of course it won't be easy. Nothing worthwhile ever is.✤

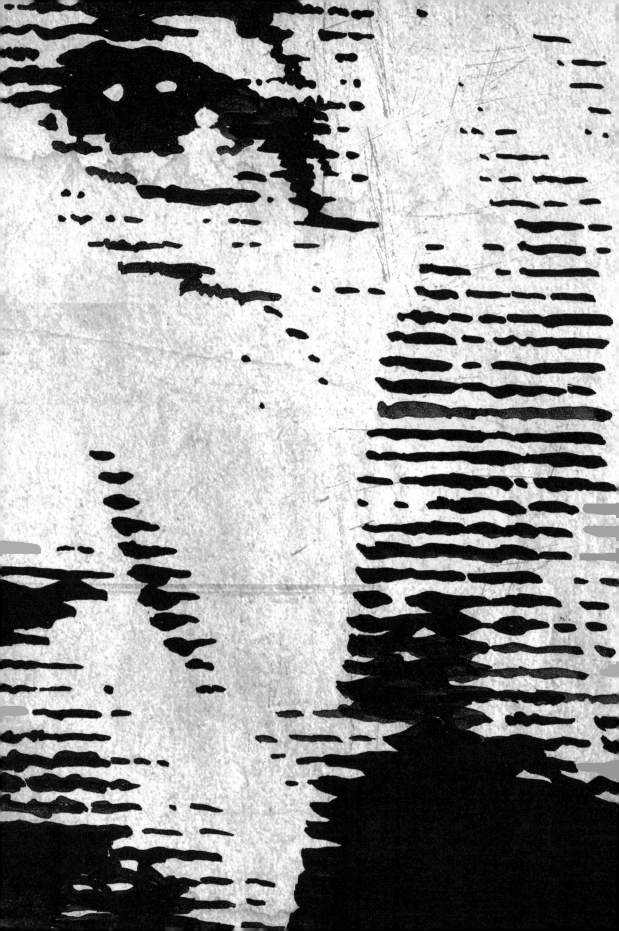

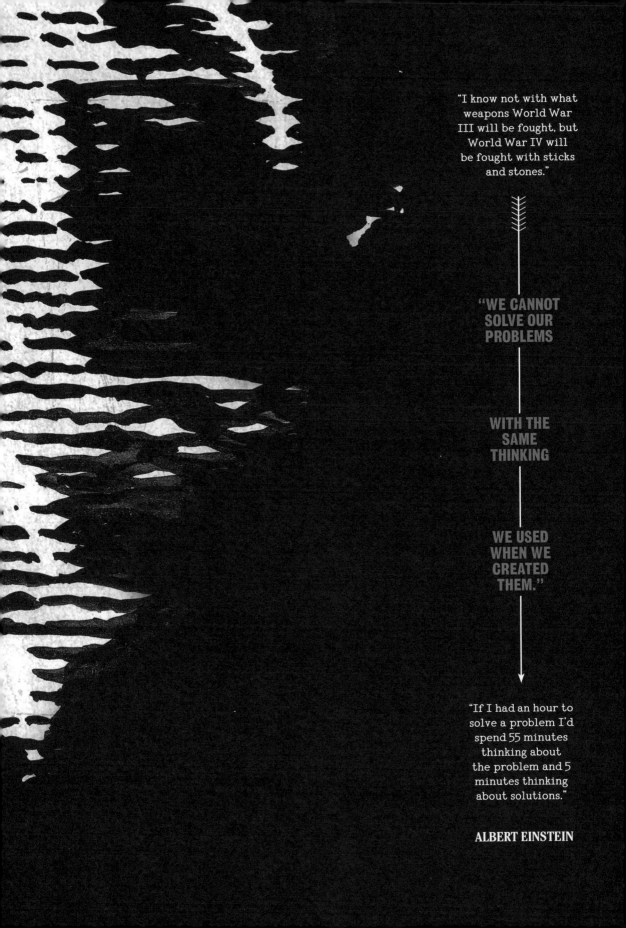

"I know not with what weapons World War III will be fought, but World War IV will be fought with sticks and stones."

"WE CANNOT SOLVE OUR PROBLEMS

WITH THE SAME THINKING

WE USED WHEN WE CREATED THEM."

"If I had an hour to solve a problem I'd spend 55 minutes thinking about the problem and 5 minutes thinking about solutions."

ALBERT EINSTEIN

THE REALITY OF THE SITUATION AND THE SITUATION OF REALITY

JEFF DENKINS

SURVIVALIST: AMSTERDAM, NETHERLANDS

You've been battling the elements, where have you been?

I get a form of arthritis and potentially I need to go on some quite strong drugs to deal with that and as part of that process I needed to get check ups and they found a lymph node which was enlarged and I immediately started thinking that I had some form of cancer. It just spiralled out of control. Three very qualified doctors said "you are fine" but for some reason it went from there that everything was making me anxious and I started analysing how I could get out of this and started questioning my own thoughts.

I thought about it the whole time and I felt extremely anxious, with physical symptoms of anxiety; waking up shaking from a nightmare. Butterflies, falling off a cliff type of thing, feeling absolutely terrible. That is what my anxiety was like. You are on the edge of a cliff and you have that fear that you are going to fall, like a massive piece of panic and it fluctuates a bit but at its peak that is what it feels like.

I then started seeing a psychologist and was discussing it and he was explaining to me how the mind works and how a lot of the therapies are around thought recognition and recognising that they are just thoughts and thoughts don't really have any power over you. Your thoughts determine your feelings. So thoughts and feelings are closely linked.

It's about controlling your thoughts. It was going well until I started thinking "what am I without thoughts?"

I started trying to work out how the mind works and then I thought (and this was in an extremely high level of anxiety so I couldn't necessarily think about things rationally and it really bothered me that I couldn't work out how my mind was working) "what if I don't get out of this? What if I'm going mad?"

I was questioning my sanity. Your body and your mind are separate so I started to try and rationalise "what am I without thoughts", "what is anyone without their thoughts"? But there is another part to it which is your actions. Everyone has a thought but it is the actions that are more you. Then it went one step further and I started questioning; it's all about thoughts and I don't know how I got on to that, I got on to 1:01 philosophical questions; "how do I know anything is real"? Descartes said "If I think, I exist". For some reason that became a recurring thought. I started second guessing my own mind

So I went through a process that, in a way I am still going through, I still have those thoughts but what it eventually comes back to is, does it really actually matter? And I think this is probably the biggest concern for me the fact that what I thought was certain is actually uncertain. The only way out of this is to be able to tolerate uncertainty. I can't use my logical mind to try and explain everything because I can always come up with a counter argument. I was going through a period of really battling with my mind.

I was trying to put it into perspective by saying to myself,

there must be more to a person than just their thoughts. So there has to be a part of you that's either a deeper level of who you are, like your values or your beliefs. So I think there must be something like a moral compass within you that means that you don't do certain things and it is actually the reason why it makes you anxious sometimes because your thoughts are straying away from you. So it's not until you realise that your thoughts don't control you that you can find some peace.

"I WAS QUESTIONING MY SANITY."

Beneath the thoughts at a subconscious level there are values or a moral compass or something. There has got to be something deeper, than just the day to day, influenced by your environment, what is happening around you and where you are working.

I can definitely see how people get caught up in their thoughts and ultimately I think that is when people have a mental illness, which is actually the fear I had for myself, it's because they can't distance themselves from their thoughts.

Because I've had to question my own sanity, I've had to confront questions such as the meaning of life and how it all works.

I think that because I'm coming out the other side, I can look at this as having been a tough journey to go through but an enlightening one also. ❖

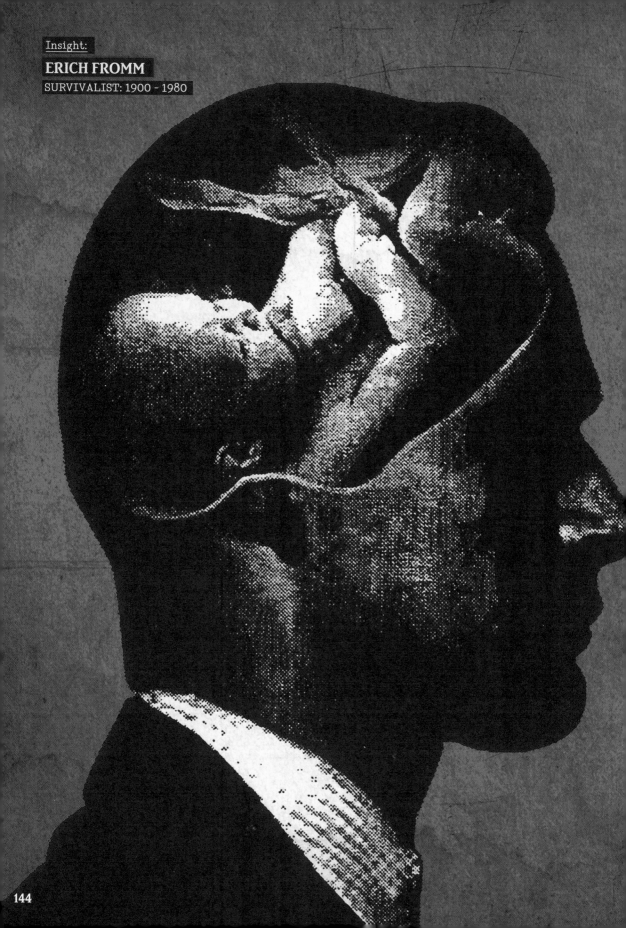

SENSE OF SELF

German-American psychoanalyst Erich Fromm believed that the best way to survive the harsh realities of modern life is to find meaning through the construction and birth of an "authentic self".

According to Fromm, the desire to hunt meaning in our lives, is the defining characteristic of humankind.

Our greatest blessing as human beings is also our biggest curse, according to Fromm: Our awareness that we exist. Fromm observed that we are "Life being aware of itself."

Fromm thought that our ability to reason (although highly useful, in terms of surviving in a harsh and chaotic world), also "makes us aware of our own mortality and the mortality of our loved ones. This understanding creates a chronic source of tension and an unbearable loneliness that we are always seeking to overcome."

It is this tension that, as we have learnt from the Big Game Hunters earlier in our journey, compels us to search for meaning in our lives. This, according to Fromm, is a defining characteristic of humankind.

"Although life is inherently painful, we can make it bearable by giving it meaning through pursuing and constructing an authentic self. The ultimate aim of life is to develop what Fromm described as "the most precious quality man is endowed with – the love of life".

It is this love of life – being true to oneself, and finding a sense of purpose that can help a disconnected individual overcome their "sense of isolation and alienation."

Fromm believed that "It is imperative to discover one's own independent sense of self, and one's own personal views and value systems, rather than adhering to conventional or authoritarian norms."

Just as we heard earlier on our journey from another hunter, Fromm reasons that "If we try to hand responsibility for our choices to other people or institutions we become alienated from ourselves, when the very purpose of our lives is to define ourselves through embracing our personal uniqueness, discovering our own ideas and abilities, and embracing that which differentiates each of us from other people."

Fromm sums it up, saying "Man's main task is to give birth to himself. In doing so, he frees himself from confusion, loneliness, and apathy."

His ideas are important to the central theme of this very book, as he links the importance of creativity, to the task of finding meaning.

In our own life, "we can achieve this by following our own ideas and passions, and through creative purpose, because 'creativity requires the courage to let go of certainties'."

Perhaps the most significant lesson we can learn from Erich Fromm, is that the purpose of creativity is not merely for any superficial pursuit. But is fundamental to the very essence of humanity, and is quite likely the most important weapon any hunter has to survive with, in this brutal existence, we call life. ✤

REVOLU

How do revolutions begin? Throughout history they've followed a distinct pattern which begins with population becoming aware that their leadership may not have the best interests of the people at heart.

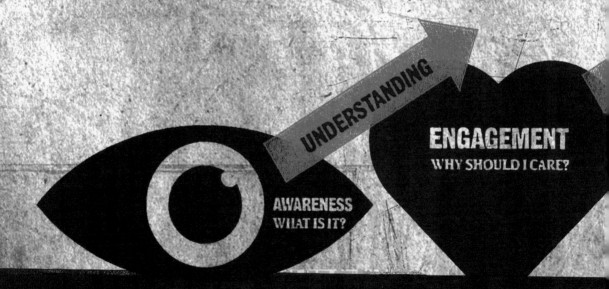

UNDERSTANDING

ENGAGEMENT
WHY SHOULD I CARE?

AWARENESS
WHAT IS IT?

Author Naomi Wolf tracks authoritarian trends in contemporary America against a ten step "blueprint" (see sidebar) which she says was crafted by Mussolini and adopted by leftist and rightist totalitarian regimes throughout the twentieth century and into the twenty-first. She argues that more Americans are becoming aware that many freedoms are being systematically eroded.

Awareness transforms into emotional engagement once the actual state of affairs is understood. For some, it is through personal experience. For others, it is the principle of the matter - that freedoms are a right, not a privilege.

TION

ACTION

WHAT DO I DO ABOUT IT?

COMMITMENT

A tipping point is arrived at, where the idea that something is not quite right becomes so powerful that something must be done about the current situation. The idea spreads rapidly through the population. This is the moment where the concept of revolution transforms from an idea into real, direct action.✣

TEN STEPS TO CLOSING DOWN AN OPEN SOCIETY. NAOMI WOLF.

☑ 1. Invoke a terrifying internal and external enemy
Terrorist sleeper cells / ISIS, Al Qaeda, Taliban.

☑ 2. Create a gulag
Guantánamo Ba.y

☑ 3. Develop a thug caste
Private armed 'Security' contractors fill this role.

☑ 4. Set up an internal surveillance system
NSA, CIA, INR, DIA, DHS ETC. ETC. ETC.

☑ 5. Harass citizens' groups
"A little-noticed new law has redefined activism such as animal rights protests as "terrorism". So the definition of "terrorist" slowly expands to include the opposition.

☑ 6. Engage in arbitrary detention and release
"Black Americans are statistically more likely to be subjected to this treatment".

☑ 7. Target key individuals
Julian Assange, Edward Snowden.

☑ 8. Control the press
Corporatisation of the press and political influence result in media bias and propaganda.

☑ 9. Dissent equals treason
Activists and academics regularly labelled as "Un-American" under the Bush regime.

☑ 10. Suspend the rule of law
The John Warner Defence Authorization Act of 2007 gives the President powers to declare martial law during a state of emergency.

PRESSURE POINTS

The internet links billions of people together as though it were
the nervous system connecting the world as one body. Ideas
are shared and spread like impulses transmitted along neural
pathways. A person sitting in Nebraska can tweet their idea to
the world, which may resonate with someone in Johannesburg,
sparking a wave of conversation, expanding the idea and
making it more powerful.

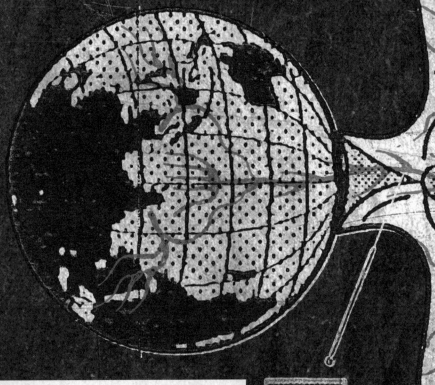

"The richest 1% of the world's population
now owns 50% of its total wealth, according
to a report by Credit Suisse." @guardian

"When so many people are dying of starvation,
is it right that so few people have so much
wealth?" @spinfluencewolf

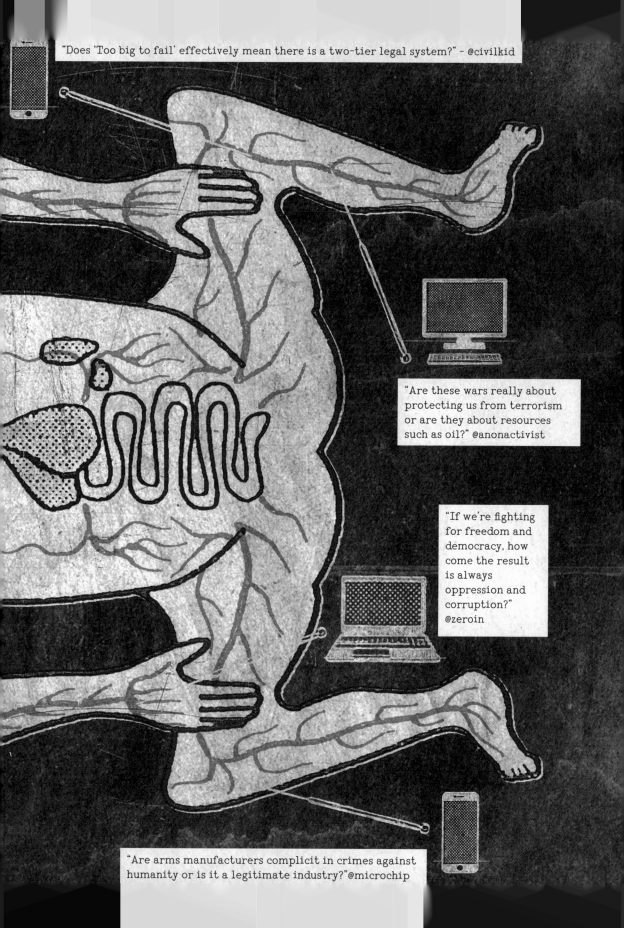

NOAM CHOMSKY
LINGUIST, PHILOSOPHER, ANARCHIST.
MASSACHUSETTS, U.S.

ANARCHY

Creative progress is usually typified by the breaking through of some kind of barrier. Whether it be a social norm, the status quo, or simply achieving something greater than was assumed possible.

Anarchist Noam Chomsky answers a few questions about the role of creativity in the world.

What is the relationship between Anarchism and Creativity?

The primary commitment of anarchism is freedom. One cannot say that freedom is a necessary prerequisite for creativity; for example, some of the most creative musical genres (blues, jazz) were created by slaves and their bitterly repressed descendants.

But it surely enhances the opportunities.

Since creativity is more or less in the service of consumerism, is capitalism a more powerful idea than creativity?

The kind of creativity that is in the service of consumerism, like advertising, seems to me an extremely shallow variant.

What is the relationship between creative and critical thinking?

They interact. ❖

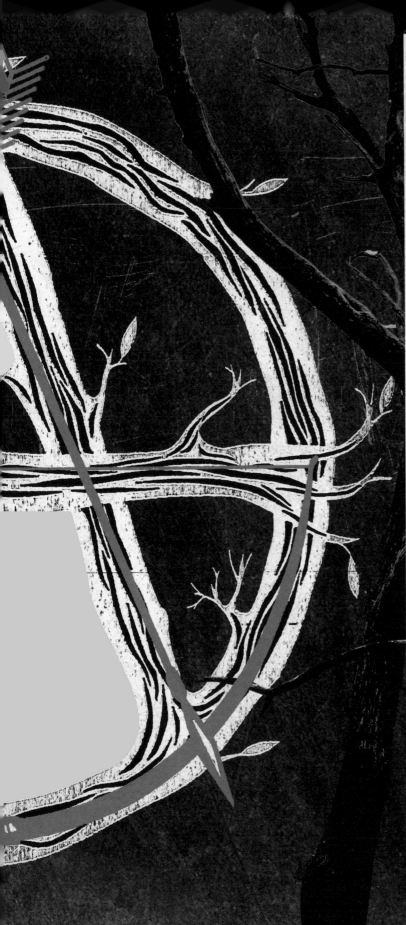

Perhaps Anarchism is a Killer Idea which could be used to challenge some of the dominant ideologies in our mental environment?

This excerpt from Noam Chomsky's book *On Anarchism* explains its purpose:

"Every form of authority and domination and hierarchy, every authoritarian structure, has to prove that it's justified - it has no prior justification. For instance, when you stop your five-year-old kid from trying to cross the street, that's an authoritarian situation: It's got to be justified. Well in that case, I think you can give a justification. But the burden of proof for any exercise of authority is always on the person exercising it - invariably. And when you look, most of these authority structures have no justification: they have no moral justification, they have no justification in the interests of the person lower in the hierarchy, or in the interests of other people, or the environment, or the future, or the society, or anything else - they're just there to preserve certain structures of power and domination, and the people at the top.

So I think that whenever you find situations of power, these questions should be asked - and the person who claims the legitimacy of the authority always bears the burden of justifying it. And if they can't justify it, it's illegitimate and should be dismantled. To tell you the truth, I don't really understand anarchism as being much more than that. As far as I can see, it's just the point of view that says people have the right to be free, and if there are constraints on that freedom then you've got to justify them." ❧

To bear the brunt
of modern life.
The hunter draws
a sharpened knife.

And cuts a path,
to find a way.
Braves the storm
'til night turns day.

Gale force winds,
one must fight.
Until the purpose
is in sight.

THE HU

NT

You set off before dawn with a spring in your step. Spirits are high and before long you find the first tracks and spoors. Your spine tingles and senses heighten. The Killer Idea is out there somewhere. The hunt has begun.

Soon you find a forest. As you venture in, thick branches conspire overhead to block out the sun. In the low light you keep your eyes close to the ground.

There are clues to be found here. You gather them
up eagerly and with each one the image of your prey
becomes a little sharper in your mind.

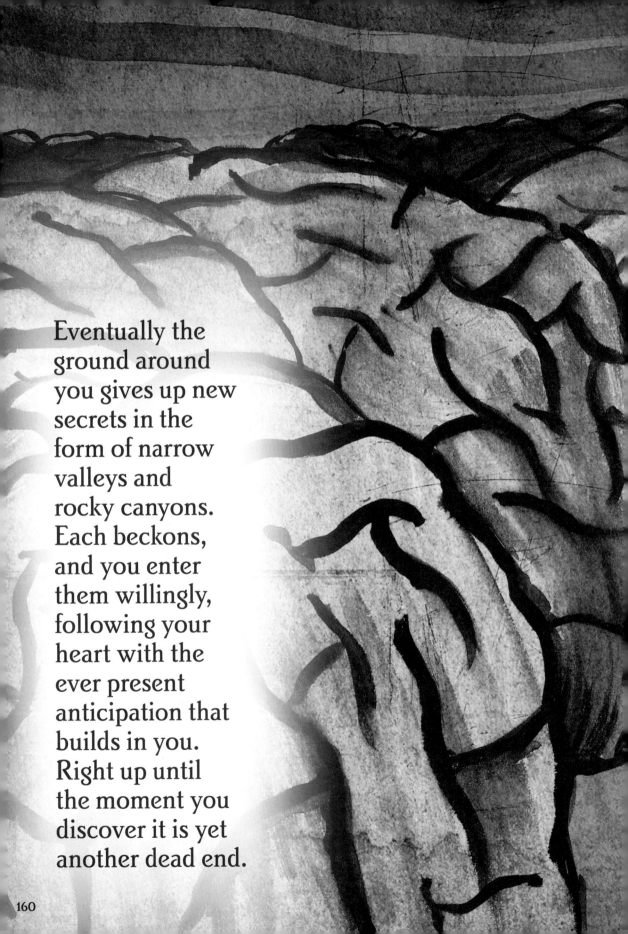

Eventually the ground around you gives up new secrets in the form of narrow valleys and rocky canyons. Each beckons, and you enter them willingly, following your heart with the ever present anticipation that builds in you. Right up until the moment you discover it is yet another dead end.

The peaks and troughs of the land ease then fade away to nothing. Your spirits sink as low as the featureless desolation you have stumbled into. Nothing lives here. You've reached the wasteland. Nervous energy propels you forward, as you realise the Killer Idea is nowhere to be seen. You move without thinking, knowing it is your only way out.

Slowly the texture of the land returns. You eagerly
welcome the uneven ground and new features, but
something else is changing. The weather takes a turn
for the worse and an angry wind whips into life.

Ideas and thought starters, once so calm and ordered in your mind, begin to swirl angrily. You put your head down, grit your teeth and keep moving. The Killer Idea is out there, you just have to ignore the chaos and keep going.

The winds of your mind die down, but in the stillness that follows you hear a new threat. The beasts of doubt have found you. High above they circle, questioning your every move. Are you on the right path? Is every step a wasted one? To look up is to question yourself. The temptation to turn back nags at you. But on you go.

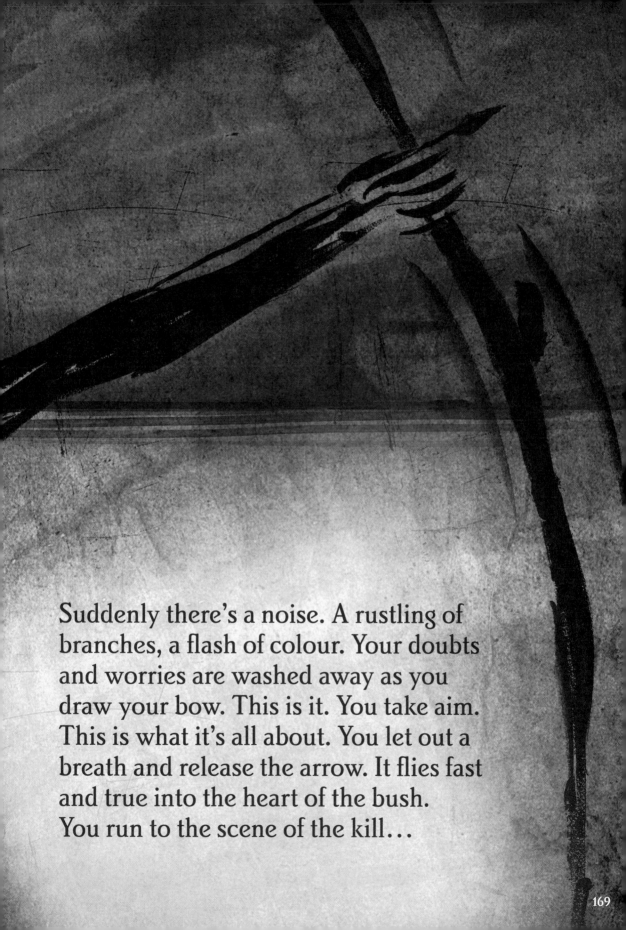

Suddenly there's a noise. A rustling of branches, a flash of colour. Your doubts and worries are washed away as you draw your bow. This is it. You take aim. This is what it's all about. You let out a breath and release the arrow. It flies fast and true into the heart of the bush. You run to the scene of the kill…

To find nothing. Was your aim off?
Or your instincts? Was the Killer Idea
even there at all? As you wrestle with
these thoughts, another greater blow
awaits you on the brow of the next hill.

Mountains and valleys stretch off into the distance.
Only now do you grasp the true nature of the challenge
you have set yourself. Behind you lies the path home.
It beckons you teasingly. In front, the great unknown.

with only the promise of more hard work. Your prize
seems further away than ever. But you cling to a faint
hope as you take the first step towards the imposing

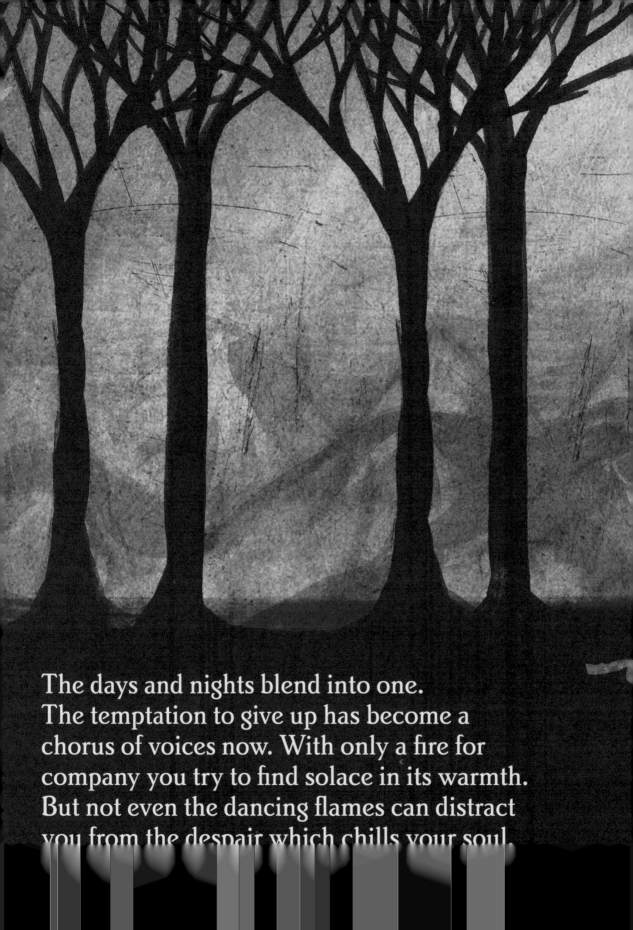

The days and nights blend into one.
The temptation to give up has become a
chorus of voices now. With only a fire for
company you try to find solace in its warmth.
But not even the dancing flames can distract
you from the despair which chills your soul.

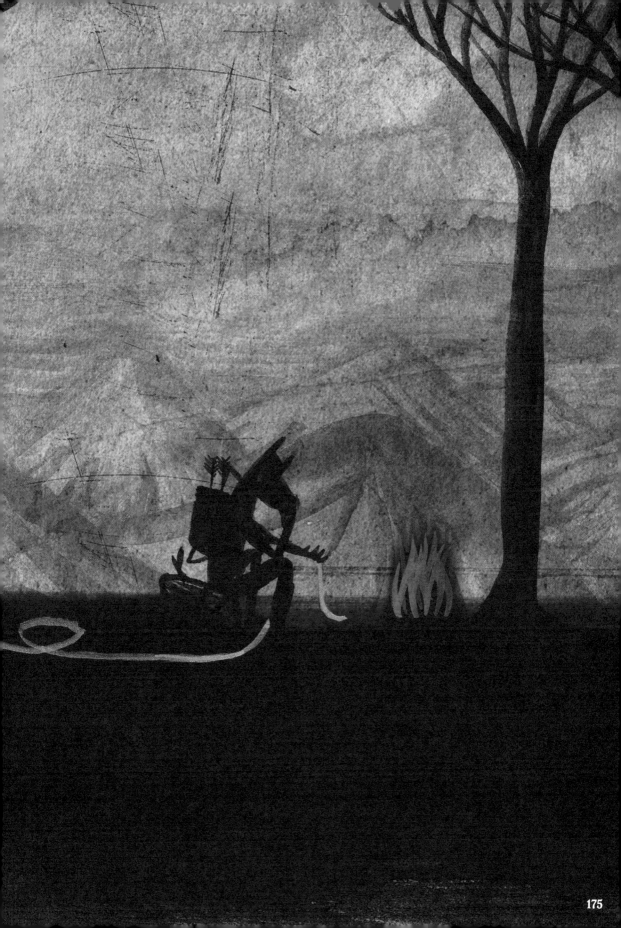

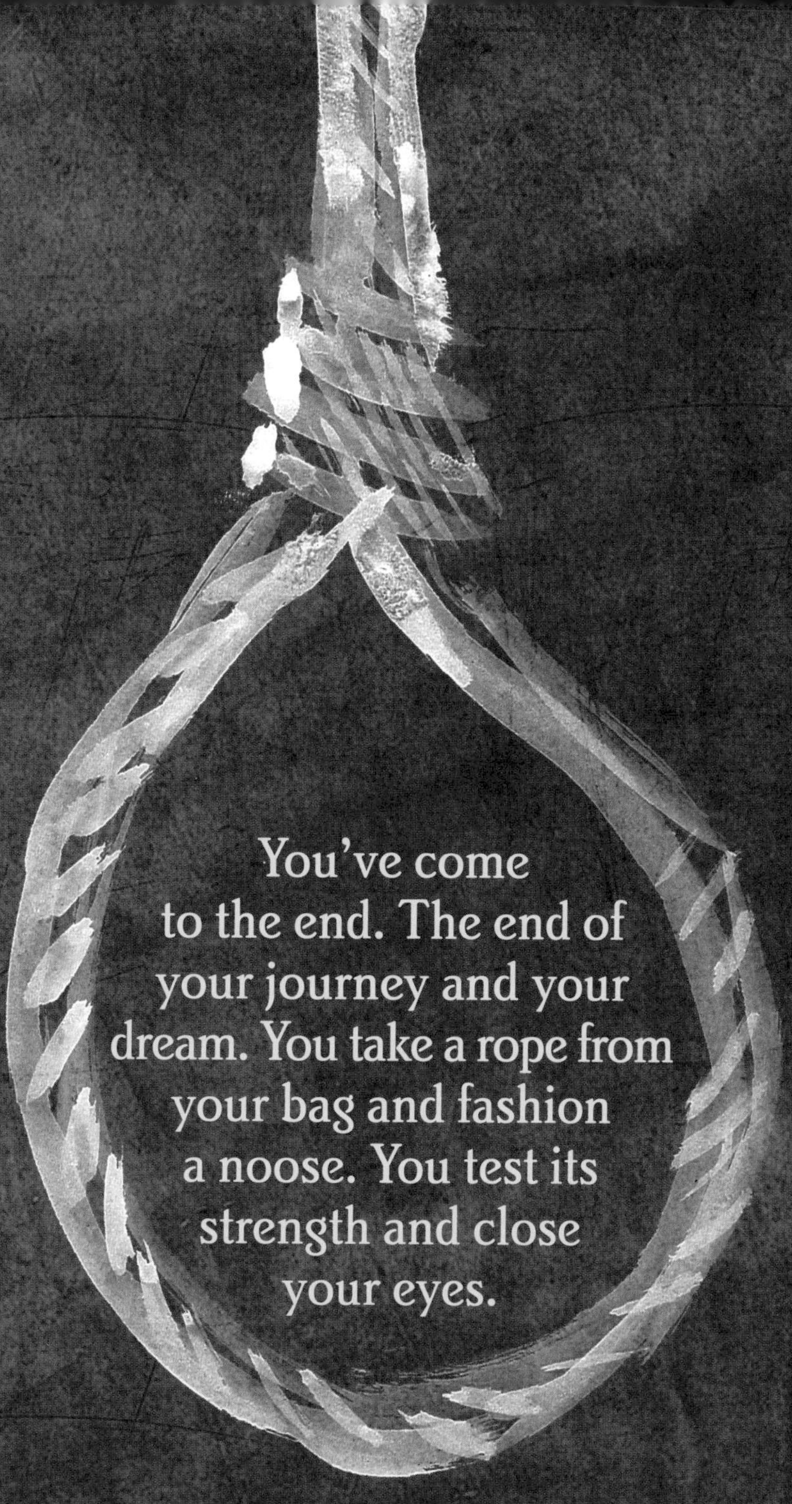

You've come
to the end. The end of
your journey and your
dream. You take a rope from
your bag and fashion
a noose. You test its
strength and close
your eyes.

From out of nowhere it appears.
The Killer Idea glides down and
lands gracefully. It stands near
the fire, lit by the dying flames.
You freeze, petrified that the
slightest movement will scare
this precious creature into the
darkness forever. But instead
it moves closer.

Right to your feet.

This is the moment you have lived and breathed for. Hidden in the struggles and doubts you have carried over countless mountains. The soul destroying climbs, the lonely cold nights when you wanted to give up. All is washed away in an instant, leaving you cleansed in this glorious moment as you look the Killer Idea in the eye. There is only one thing left to do.

THE KI

LL

You draw your knife and raise it above your head. You admire your prey one last time, knowing it will never be like this again. Then, with a blood curdling cry, you bring the blade down.

The deed is done, your adventure is over, but you know this is just the beginning for your Killer Idea.

Your final act is to set it free, to see
the fruits of your labour take flight.
This is what it was all about, sharing
your idea with the world.

The hunt has taken its toll. Your body and mind are weary, but your wounds bear testament to your refusal to give in. Your scars will serve as reminders of your belief in yourself.

The space within you, filled for so long with purpose and hope, is now an empty hole. But already you feel that void filling with memories of your journey and the prize you claimed, for while the Killer Idea belongs to the world, its soul will always remain with you.

And so it is
the hunt is done.
Now turn and face
the setting sun.

Over the land
that you did roam.
The time has come
to head back home.

But pause and watch
this sublime sight.
Your Killer Idea
is in full flight.

THE END

SO INTO THE WILD YOU GO.

BIBLIOGRAPHIE

INTO THE WILD

Page 20
Teresa Amabile, Constance
Hadley, Steve Kramer. Creativity
Under the Gun. (The Time-
Pressure/Creativity Matrix).
Harvard Business Review. 2002.

BIG GAME HUNTING

Page 36
Charles Darwin.
On Natural Selection.
Penguin, 2005.

Page 40
Hunter S. Thompson. Letters of
Note: An Eclectic Collection of
Correspondence Deserving of a
Wider Audience. Shaun Usher.
Barnes & Noble, 2013.

HUNTER GATHERERS

Page 52 - 61
James Webb Young.
A Technique for producing Ideas.
McGraw-Hill. 1939 (2003).

MOUNTAIN GUIDES

Page 68 - 71
Edward de Bono
Lateral Thinking: Creativity Step
by Step. Harper Collins, 2010.

Page 72
Edward de Bono
Six Thinking Hats
Penguin, 2010.

Page 74
Tina Seelig.
inGenius:
A Crash Course on Creativity.
HarperCollins, 2012.

TRAPPERS

Page 104
Dieter Rams.
Ten Principles for Good Design.
fastcodesign.com, 22/06/15.
Diana Budds

Page 112
Vince Frost
Design Your Life: Applying
Design Principles to your Life.
Lantern, 2015.

HEAD HUNTERS

Page 125
Dave Trott.
Make Fear Your Friend.
davetrott.campaignlive.co.uk
March 11, 2015.

Page 127
George Lois.
Damn Good Advice
(For People with Talent!).
Phaidon, 2012.

Page 129
Paul Arden.
It's Not How Good You Are,
It's How Good You Want to Be:
The World's Best Selling Book.
Phaidon, 2003.

Paul Arden.
Whatever You Think
Think the Opposite.
Phaidon, 2006.

Page 130
David Ogilvy
The Eternal Pursuit of
Unhappiness: Being very good is
no good, you have to very, very,
very, very, very good
Ogilvy & Mather Worldwide, 2009.

SURVIVALISTS

Page 145
Nigel Benson, Catherine Collin,
Joannah Ginsburg, Voula Grand,
Merrin Lazyan, Marcus Weeks.
The Psychology Book.
Dorling Kindersly, 2012

Page 146
Naomi Wolf.
Fascist America, in 10 easy steps.
Theguardian.com. 24/04/2007

INTERVIEWS

Askew one
Graffiti Artist
Interview, skype: 15/11/15

Carla Adams
Artist
Interview, email: 20/2/16

Corianna and Brianna
Coco and Breezy
Interview, email: 5/1/16

Dave Trott
Interview, email: 22/4/15

Liam Howlett
The Prodigy
Interview, skype: 9/10/15

Marina Munn
Illustrator
Interview, email: 15/2/16

Matt McAteer
Poet
Interview, skype: 21/08/15

Noam Chomsky
Massachusetts Institure of
Technology
Q&A, email: 26/5/15, 29/5/15.

Nick Onken
Photographer
Interview, email: 18/8/15

Sacha Barber
FCA
Interview, email: 18/12/15

Vince Frost
Frost Collective
Interview, skype: 30/10/15

NOTES